"I have awaited the publication of this book impatiently because it tells one of the most remarkable stories of our generation. A passionate love runs through these pages. A vision of loving people that is infectious and transforms the heart of the reader. This is a story of tears, tears of compassion that became tears of joy. Well written, full of wisdom, this story is also a handbook for a rebuilt world. Revive your own heart, learn a strategy that changes everything. Explore these pages, then join me in passing on this story to everybody you know."

John Dawson, international ambassador, YWAM Medical Ships; president emeritus, YWAM

"The Homes of Home story has changed our family's life. We have also made this story a part of our lives beyond our family. We have engaged our friends, church, local charities, youth organizations, and company in the story too. This story is the best taste of God we have ever had. Don't read this book until you're ready to be changed by God's heart for the poor. Love, give, serve, and enjoy!"

Dave and Trina Stone, cofounders and worship leaders, First Rate, Inc.

"This is the inspiring story of how God has richly blessed tens of thousands of people through Homes of Hope . . . and not just the poor. Many times I have taken my family or leadership team to build a home for a poor family. We went to transform the lives of others, but each time found that we also experienced a profound transformation. Homes of Hope is the best hands-on mission experience that I have ever done."

Kevin Jenkins, president and CEO, World Vision International

"My family and I were very moved by our experience building a home in Mexico. It has had a lasting effect on all of us, and we salute the work that Sean leads. This book captures the true spirit of his calling."

Steve Reinemund, chairman and CEO, PepsiCo (retired)

"My wife and I, kids, friends, business teams, YPO chapter and forum have been going on Homes of Hope builds around the world since 1997. The feedback is outstanding: 'Best family trip ever!' 'Best YPO event.' 'I can't believe I get to work for a company that allows us to do something this amazing!' I have experienced through Homes of Hope the joy and fulfillment that come through giving, and it's contagious! If you're looking for a life-changing adventure in our world of spandex heroes and political disappointments, this is the real deal!"

Mike Kemper, former CEO, NPL Construction Co.; cofounder, chairman, and president, Canadian Utility Construction Corp

"I am honored to be Sean and Janet Lambert's pastor as well as their friend. After twenty years of observing the Lamberts up close, I would use three words to describe them: humble, faithful, and visionary. The fruit of their humility and faithfulness to the vision God gave them birthed the Homes of Hope movement, which has impacted thousands of lives around the world. This is an inspiring story and also a great example of what God desires to do through all his people who, like the Lamberts, will simply be willing to live out the call of Micah 6:8 'to do justly, to love mercy, and to walk humbly with your God' (NKJV)."

Pastor Bruce Greeco, Summit Church San Diego

"We have been blessed to build homes with Homes of Hope for thirteen years. Every build is exciting. Building with our children and friends, the family, the YWAM staff, and other volunteers is a deeply fulfilling and even spiritual event. It gives us the opportunity to be the hands and feet of Christ, and it is a blessing to know that we have made a difference in the life of the family for whom we are building."

Robert Murchison, president, Murchison Capital Partners, L.P.

"Take time to savor this rich treasure. Along the way you will learn about a ministry that started with a $1000 offering and with God's help became a ten-talent organization. Having participated in a dozen home builds myself, and knowing the founders personally, I can say with all sincerity this story is a must-read. And if you haven't built a home for the poor yet, sign up soon and help write the next chapter of this ongoing story."

Bob Westfall, CEO, The Westfall Group

"I still see the faces and the flowing tears of the many families as we handed them the keys to their new home. Over a forty-eight-hour time span, the impoverished family's life transitions from living on a dirt floor in a flimsy structure susceptible to the elements, into a dry, safe, cozy home with a solid concrete floor. The impact goes well beyond the recipient family. As a business owner, it affords an incomparable bonding experience for my partners and their families. One of my CEOs told me, 'I learned more about my new executive team during this two-day build than I had learned in two years with my former company.' The experience of building homes for the poor is the closest I've come to looking into the eyes of God."

John C. Tlapek, president, Summit Equity Group

"Our two daughters, ages twelve and nine at the time, *very* reluctantly did their first Homes of Hope trip, saying, 'Oh Dad, do we really have to go?' Upon their return they raced to their rooms and phones and computers to tell their friends what an amazing trip they had, how fortunate they are, and how much they helped another family. No parent could ask for more than to see their family blessed by helping others. Read this book, take your family, change lives!"

Eric Affeldt, CEO, ClubCorp

"What difference can one weekend make? As a pastor of a large church, I have had the privilege of convincing hundreds of individuals, in forty-plus trips with Homes of Hope, that serving a family in need will forever change one's perspective on God's love and the role we can play in it. And they are never disappointed. Hope given away is returned to the giver in greater measure. Mankind's capacity to love our neighbor is far greater than we realize. Be inspired by this story and the seemingly foolish steps of faith that led to thousands of lives being transformed."

Lee Coate, executive pastor, The Crossing Church, Las Vegas

"I have found that a compelling story embedded with life-giving principles changes lives. Homes of Hope is one of those compelling stories. But be careful—in reading it, you may find yourself joining the Homes of Hope movement just like I did. Their story will touch you, and their mission will inspire you. Read it today!"

Jon Gordon, author of *The Energy Bus* and *The Carpenter*

"One of the highlights of my life occurred on a trip to build houses for the poor with Homes of Hope in Mexico. What sheer delight to build a complete house from the ground up with my daughter and other families—and then watch the eruption of joy from the family who were given the keys to their first home. Homes of Hope not only exemplifies a well-run humanitarian organization, but it links the love of Christ to practical Christian service. As you read this compelling story, watch out, because your heart may pull you to pick up a hammer and join with their grand vision!"

Bruce Wilkinson, president, Teach Every Nation

"*The Homes of Hope Story* has given us a look into an amazing mission that has helped thousands, given purpose to thousands more, and started a global movement to house the poor. We all have a short time on earth and want to fill our lives with purpose while we are here. Sean has been blessed to live with purpose and guide a multitude to this calling. If you want inspiration to grow impact in your company and your life—read this book."

Jim Schleckser, author of *Great CEOs Are Lazy*; CEO, Inc. CEO Project

"Homes of Hope once again proves that those things that transform our world and make it a better place almost always begin with one small act, one little idea that gets set into motion. As you read this amazing story, contemplate two things: (1) how to engage with Homes of Hope so that you too will experience this life-changing opportunity, and (2) how to pursue and act on that idea, dream, or vision you have to make the world a better place."

Ray Hilbert, cofounder, Truth At Work; international best-selling author

"Every year thousands of Mexican families stream into Tijuana dreaming of a new and better life. They struggle to make ends meet, and many lose hope along the way. As a family we have found that participation in Homes of Hope not only changed the lives of the poor, but it has changed our lives as well. Sean and Janet and their team of dedicated volunteers freely share God's love with everyone they meet. Read this book, be inspired, and discover for yourself why it's more blessed to give than to receive."

David and Lise Ash, Langley, British Columbia

"Participation in Homes of Hope has taught us a very practical and real theology in that God has a huge heart to bless the poor. When you give to the poor, you are doing God's work. When you do God's work, you meet God. When you meet God, you get to know him. When you get to know him, you have the opportunity to develop a deeper relationship with him. It has been a privilege to work with and support Sean and Janet and the entire Lambert family as they have so tirelessly devoted their lives to helping the poor. If you have not yet been part of the Homes of Hope experience, don't delay—book a trip, bring your family and those you care about. You may come with the great intention of helping others, but you will depart with a much greater and indescribable gift."

Robert and Jill Kulhawy, founders, YPO Homes of Hope, Calgary, Alberta

"Sean and Janet Lambert are our heroes. We've watched them for twenty-four years build Homes of Hope, and they are the real deal."

Jane Crane, Founder, Adopt A Widow

"Homes of Hope has had a wonderfully positive impact on our family. We love it so much that one or more of our family members have participated in thirty-four Homes of Hope experiences. We have seen Homes of Hope change lives among those who receive a home and also among those who go to build."

Chris Crane, founder, Edify.org

"Each year for the last fifteen years our family has participated in the Homes of Hope program. After every build we have gone home feeling more blessed than when we arrived. Sean and Janet and their staff have done a fantastic job showing the least of these the love of Jesus. I hope this book inspires you to form your own team and discover for yourself the joy of serving the poor."

Chuck Anderson, founder, Bandera Ventures

"As a builder myself, I know the importance of people having shelter—a safe place they can call 'home.' Homes of Hope has recalibrated my thinking about how to help the poor in this endeavor. Not only have I participated in Homes of Hope builds, I also served on their board of directors for eight years and helped guide the ministry through some of its biggest growth challenges. You will enjoy reading this book, but you will even more enjoy participating in a Homes of Hope build for yourself. It will definitely change your life for the better!"

Tom Wermers, CEO, Wermers Companies

"These days it seems people are searching for significance but in their quest are losing sight of impact. Sean and Janet Lambert, through Homes of Hope, are enjoying an abundance of both. I have had the privilege of building two Homes of Hope, and on both my trips I have experienced the true and guiltless joy that comes from serving the poor. My faith informs me that the poor are much greater than the rich—not only in number but in priority to God. If true, then it stands to reason that their voice should be one of the clearest, most influential voices on the earth. *The Homes of Hope Story* is the voice of the poor front and center. Their voice is beautiful, and it calls us to a life of service. I'm grateful for Sean and his obedience to write this book. May it lead us to lives of service, significance, and impact."

Hunter Smith, singer-songwriter for Hunter Smith Band, author of *The Jersey Effect*, Super Bowl XLI champion

"Over the past few years hundreds of Olympic and professional athletes have built scores of Homes of Hope through Hope Sports, a nonprofit organization I started after being inspired by Sean Lambert, the founder of Homes of Hope. As a professional cyclist myself, I understood the emptiness of living only to win the next race. Participation in Homes of Hope is a game changer for athletes, and it helps them discover the joy and fulfillment of giving. Sean Lambert was not the only person that inspired me; after meeting his daughter Andrea, I decided she was the one I wanted to spend the rest of my life with, and we got married. Together we are committed to inspire athletes to bring hope to the world."

Guy East, founder, Hope Sports

"Nowhere in all of my travels around the world have I encountered a clearer vision of God's kingdom at work than with Homes of Hope. This program has brought hope to thousands of impoverished families by providing them permanent shelter and by demonstrating God's love to them in a tangible way. The Homes of Hope experience is so powerful that it has brought some of the toughest athletes I know to tears. God has used the Lambert family's small steps of obedience to make a big impact in the world. Read the book and be inspired—it's a compelling and entertaining story."

Ben King, professional cyclist, Tour de France rider, 2014

"One of the biggest lies that elite athletes face is that their self-worth is based in athletic performance. This pressure can lead to a self-centered life that lacks community and fulfillment. The simple but transformative act of building a home for an impoverished family challenges self-focus and connects athletes to a greater purpose. This act of generosity no doubt changes the future of a well-deserving family, but it also inspires athletes to live more meaningful lives as they experience the power of unconditional love. The beauty of what Sean Lambert started with Homes of Hope that inspired the creation of Hope Sports is everyone leaves changed."

Dr. Ben Houltberg, associate professor of human development, Fuller Theological Seminary

"In over thirty years of working with Olympic and professional athletes, I have never seen a program as effective as Homes of Hope for inspiring, challenging and transforming an athlete's life. Elite competition requires intensive self-focus and all that self-focus can easily take its toll, numbing athletes to their need for relationships. Homes of Hope in partnership with Hope Sports gives these elite competitors an opportunity to make a concrete and life-transforming difference to a family in need. As they work alongside the parents and their children, they become included in the family's circle of love, the athletes discover something deep within themselves coming alive—their need for and utter joy from reaching out and touching others. When the home is finished, both the athletes and the family are in tears, their lives permanently changed."

Reverend Canon Doctor John Ashley Null, US Olympic chaplain

"Jesus admonishes us to 'care for the poor and the least of our brothers and sisters,' giving them shelter in their time of need (Matt. 25:35–40). Homes of Hope has been doing this on four continents for decades. Thousands of impoverished families now have their own beautiful home, personal dignity, and shelter from inclement weather and thievery. By this one generous provision, their lives have changed dramatically. Also changed are all the volunteers who have used their own funds, personal energy, and skills to go serve the poor, as Darlene and I have done, as well as our children and grandchildren. Read Sean's book and get involved. You, your family, your church, and your business will be transformed as well."

Loren and Darlene Cunningham, founders, Youth With A Mission

"The Lamberts' story truly brings to life Jesus's promise that it is indeed better to give than to receive. The Lambert family and many thousands of lives have been touched by this magnificent display of miracle of miracles. This book shows that the unbelievable becomes believable when we together serve the poor and change the world in such a positive way with unconditional love always. Can there be a greater purpose in our lives?"

Sam Kolias, CEO, Boardwalk REIT

"Homes of Hope is the best *family* mission trip in the world! We should know—after sending over six thousand of our employees and their families to build over three hundred homes for the poor, we are the ones who have been blessed. Sean and Janet, along with their team, helped us transition from a giving company to a company of givers!"

Dave and Jessica Lindsey, founders, Defenders

"Doing good in the name of Christ has always involved both sharing the gospel and helping the physical needs of those in want. Sean Lambert's book is an inspiring narrative of how his and his wife Janet's ministry has integrated both of these themes seamlessly. You will learn lots of life lessons for your own growth as well. Highly recommended."

Dr. John Townsend, *New York Times* best-selling author; founder, The Townsend Institute of Leadership and Counseling

"Homes of Hope is an incredible service experience for you, your family, or your business associates to go on. Building for the poor is a life-changing experience not just for the family receiving the house but for those who come to serve as well."

David Browne, CEO, LensCrafters (retired)

"Homes of Hope has changed a countless number of lives, including mine. The tangible product they provide in the form of a home for a family in need, while important, pales in comparison to the spiritual and emotional impact left on both the recipients and builders of the home. I am thankful for Sean Lambert and his commitment to such an awesome cause!"

Shawn Johnson East, Olympic Gold Medalist 2008

"My good friend Chris Crane 'dragged' me down to Tijuana in 1993 to build a home for the poor with YWAM. I was very sure that it would be my one and only time. God had a much different plan, as I have now completed more than seventy-five Homes of Hope trips, and I will continue to build as long as I am able. I have led home-building trips for people of all faith expressions, including family, friends, business groups, YPO chapters, churches, and inner-city kids. The joy of serving the poor is so fulfilling that my wife and I decided to get married in Tijuana after we had completed five new homes for the poor with family and friends around us. To say that serving the poor has transformed my life would be a vast understatement. While building that first home, I began to discover my true identity in Christ and what would become the most important purpose for my life—serving the poor in his name."

Steve James, carpenter, painter, electrician, roofer, and former CEO

"*The Homes of Hope Story* is not just a wonderful book; it is at once a fascinating tale of entrepreneurship, a joyful guide for building a nonprofit, and more than anything else, an inspiring lesson in obeying the Lord's call to serve 'the least of our brothers.' What makes it particularly powerful is the tangible, realistic nature of Sean's story. Homes of Hope is about real people trusting God enough to take one small step at a time, and knowing that He will turn those small steps into something great for His honor and glory. This story has changed me, my family, and my company in profound ways. Read it, and don't be afraid to take a small step of your own."

Patrick Lencioni, author of *The Advantage* and *The Five Dysfunctions of a Team*

"It matters to this one..."

THE HOMES OF HOPE STORY

Sean Lambert
with
Adam Mitchell

YWAM PUBLISHING
Seattle, Washington

YWAM Publishing is the publishing ministry of Youth With A Mission (YWAM), an international missionary organization of Christians from many denominations dedicated to presenting Jesus Christ to this generation. To this end, YWAM has focused its efforts in three main areas: (1) training and equipping believers for their part in fulfilling the Great Commission (Matthew 28:19), (2) personal evangelism, and (3) mercy ministry (medical and relief work).

For a free catalog of books and materials, call (425) 771-1153 or (800) 922-2143. Visit us online at www.ywampublishing.com.

To the poor of our world whose daily cry for help often goes unnoticed by a busy and self-consumed world.

And to the tens of thousands of people who chose to answer the call to love their neighbor and joined the Homes of Hope movement.

"For I was hungry and you gave me something to eat, I was thirsty and you gave me something to drink, I was a stranger and you invited me in, I needed clothes and you clothed me, I was sick and you looked after me, I was in prison and you came to visit me. . . . Truly I tell you, whatever you did for one of the least of these brothers and sisters of mine, you did for me."
Matthew 25:35–40

"Whoever is kind to the poor lends to the Lord,
and he will reward them for what they have done."
Proverbs 19:17

Contents

Foreword

Many years ago I participated in my first Homes of Hope build with Sean Lambert and his committed band of world changers in Baja, Mexico. It was such a moving experience I did it again, this time bringing along some folks from my company. I wanted them to feel the joy that comes from working together toward the incredible goal of building a real home for a family in need. The experience touched everyone so much that we arranged another build trip the following year.

In my years of teaching business leaders all over the world, I have found that those who understand and embrace servant leadership principles come out ahead every time—and so do their people. The most successful businesses and nonprofits become great because they understand and apply these principles. Jesus Christ, the greatest leadership role model of all time, gave freely of himself for the benefit of the whole world. Not only was Jesus a servant leader, but he was also a developer of people—he took a bunch of ordinary folks and shaped them into world changers.

The Homes of Hope Story is a book about leadership formation. Within these pages you will read about a nineteen-year-old who dropped out of college to follow the teachings of Jesus and make a difference in the world. It's a story about the poor and their cry for help. It's also a story of people who responded to the cry by joining the Homes of Hope movement. The story is told through the eyes of Sean, but you will also recognize the hand of God on his wife, Janet. And you will be inspired by his daughter, Andrea, who at three years old asked a simple question that launched the Homes of Hope movement.

Sean, Janet, and their wonderful Youth With A Mission staff have given their lives to serve the poor—and their approach has created a pathway of engagement for thousands of people who, like me, had been mere spectators. They inspire us to get out of our seats and go onto the playing field with them. They make the act of loving our neighbors into a fulfilling adventure—one I highly recommend to you, your family, and your organization.

I hope this book encourages you to discover for yourself the richness of serving God and the poor—and the joy of giving.

KEN BLANCHARD
Chief spiritual officer of The Ken Blanchard Companies
Coauthor of *The New One Minute Manager*® and *Lead Like Jesus*

Introduction

In May 1990 my three-year-old daughter, Andrea, accompanied me as I traveled with a group of eighteen other staff from Youth With A Mission Los Angeles with a simple vision to build a single house for a Mexican family in need. YWAM (pronounced "why-wham") is one of the largest interdenominational mission organizations in the world, working in more than 180 countries with a goal to "know God and make him known."[1] At the time of my first house build, I had been in YWAM for twelve years and was passionate about serving God and others.

As our group worked, hammered, and painted in the hot sun in Tijuana, Mexico, I caught a glimpse of a family living in an old abandoned bus pitched on a nearby hill. Andrea soon started playing with the other children from the area, including a set of twin sisters who were living in the rundown bus. On the second day of the build, Andrea tugged at the sleeve of my shirt with a look of concern on her face. She asked me a question that would change the course of our family's life and thousands of other lives in the years to come.

"Daddy, are you going to build a house for the bus people too?"

My daughter's question deeply touched my heart and continued to echo in my mind as our team returned home to Los Angeles after the build. During my many prior trips to Baja, Mexico, I had been continually struck by the lack of adequate shelter and sheer human need in the basics of life. All of us are created in God's image, and therefore all have great value. I knew in my heart that it was not God's intent for people to live in ramshackle shelters made out of scrap wood, plastic tarps, and cardboard. I recognized there was a tremendous opportunity

---

1. To find out more about Youth With A Mission around the world, go to www.ywam.org.

to provide shelter for the poor and, in this act of loving servanthood, to affirm their value as God's image bearers. Compassion is a powerful motivator, and the more I thought about their impoverished living conditions, the more I realized our home build wasn't intended by God to be a one-time occurrence. We may have completed construction on the single house, but our work certainly wasn't finished. It felt like the beginning of something much bigger.

I couldn't get the family living in the bus out of my thoughts. God was using Andrea's question to challenge my own apathy. Her question motivated me to return with another group of volunteers to Tijuana to construct a home for the "bus people." Her question also served as the inspiration to establish Homes of Hope, a ministry of YWAM devoted to building homes for the poor.

I believe God had it in his heart from the beginning to multiply the program and make an impact on thousands of the poor around the world. In my journey of serving others, there would be many tests, trials, and failures. God truly sustained me and intervened at key moments of my life. He gave me grace in the tough periods and joy in the breakthrough times. Overcoming obstacles increased my faith and understanding of what it meant to be a successful servant leader.

As the founder of Homes of Hope, my personal experience is deeply embedded in the story, but it is not the story itself. My wife, Janet, is the cofounder of Homes of Hope, and it was her partnership with me that helped lay its foundations. Also, I consider myself fortunate for having been able to share this incredible experience with more than 110,000 people (and growing) who have volunteered to serve the poor.

Through Homes of Hope, the faceless poor become real people and the volunteer builders become like family. By loving our neighbors in this way, we see how a home is so much more than four walls and a roof. Every Homes of Hope project is a deeply spiritual experience, and every poor family served has the opportunity to receive two houses on the dedication day: a temporary earthly home and an eternal, heavenly one. After all, it's the Father's love that draws us all in and invites us to dwell in his home forever.

During Homes of Hope's first full year in 1991 we built twelve houses, and the next year that number doubled. It took us twelve years to see the first one thousand homes built, but only four years after that to see the next thousand. In May 2015, Homes of Hope celebrated its twenty-fifth anniversary and completed construction on our 5,140th home! Today, as we move forward, we are on pace to build one thousand homes globally every two years.

There is a wonderful joy in knowing that Homes of Hope has created an opportunity for volunteers to do much more than simply write a check to a charity. The first few hundred homes were built by high school students from a variety of churches. Soon the movement grew to include volunteer teams made up of family and friends, as well as business groups and professional athletes. The economic engine that funds Homes of Hope comes from the visiting groups that come to serve. They get the joy of both paying for and building a home for a family in need. The Homes of Hope builds are open to all, no matter their beliefs or background. Our common ground is that we love the poor and want to make a difference in their lives. Everyone is welcome, and as I often say, "Any friend of the poor is a friend of mine."

What started as a single home build in the dusty hills of Tijuana, Mexico, has today blossomed into a global housing movement impacting twenty-three countries and growing. This act of giving and serving is not only personally fulfilling but also incredibly contagious. As Janet likes to say, "Homes of Hope is a gateway drug to missions. Participation is addicting, and once you build one home for the poor, be careful, you may find yourself needing another Homes of Hope fix!"

This is the story of how we couldn't stop after building just one home. It is a "we" story, as it involves thousands of people who have showed up and joined in serving those in need. It's about listening to God and obeying him and having faith when you don't know what the ultimate outcome will be. It's about the power of servant leadership, loving people unconditionally, and choosing to make a difference one person, one family, one community at a time.

ONE

Engaging a Broken World

"God is in the slums, in the cardboard boxes where the poor play house. God is in the silence of a mother who has infected her child with a virus that will end both their lives. God is in the cries heard under the rubble of war. God is in the debris of wasted opportunity and lives, and God is with us if we are with them."

Bono

S A M smiled and pointed her finger at me. "So why did you and Janet come down to Mexico years ago?" Our group of seventeen senior leaders of YWAM San Diego/Baja had gathered to clarify the *why* of our Homes of Hope ministry vision, but the directness of her question caught me off guard. We had already spent four hours in discussion around the big *why* question, and it was harder to answer than we thought. We had spent most of our time telling each other *how* we did things or *what* we did, not truly getting to our *why*.

Over the years I've heard stories of so many ministry and business leaders who lost their way because they lacked clarity about their corporate vision. Knowing the organizational *why* helps groups focus on their core purpose. It strips away potential distractions and side roads, helping them stay relevant as an organization.

Remember Blockbuster? It had fifty million loyal customers in 2004 but went bankrupt in 2010. This industry giant was supplanted by Netflix, which started out in 1998 delivering DVDs via the mail into people's homes. The majority of Blockbuster's senior leaders believed they were a retail company that answered *how* they got videos into people's homes. Netflix, however, saw themselves as being an in-the-home entertainment business, so whether it was mailing DVDs or eventually streaming content over the Internet, the *why* was what mattered. Mailing and streaming is *how* they achieved their *why*. Netflix now has over eighty million global customers!

Sam's question lingered in my mind as discussion resumed at tables around the room. So my earnest British coworker leaned in a second time, looked me in the eye, and asked, "Sean, why did you come here? Why did you recruit all of us to come here?"

I leaned back against the hard plastic chair and ran my fingers through my gray hair. I was nineteen years old when I left home in Minnesota to join Youth With A Mission, intent on trying to change the world. I was now fifty-six, and so much had happened in those thirty-seven years. I thought of all the volunteers who had joined us to engage our broken world, serving as instruments of God's generosity to the poor. That was it. I turned to Sam and said, "To engage a broken world with God's generosity." Sam smiled, looking pleased to have elicited a thoughtful answer.

My wife, Janet, who was sitting at a different table, spoke up. "Say that again. That sounded good."

Now filled with emotion, I repeated it loud enough so everyone could hear. "To engage a broken world with God's generosity." There was a pregnant pause in the room as everyone digested the summary statement. One by one they started chiming in their agreement. We had defined our why.

Over the years I had seen so many lives changed by experiencing God's generosity in a time of need. Families were overcome with joy when we gave them the keys to their new home. After building thousands of homes for the poor, I am often asked if I have a construction background. The answer is no. The truth is that I started building homes for the poor because I saw it was a great way to rebuild broken lives. We serve a generous God who loves all of his creation. Every time we build a home for the poor, I feel closer to God and experience the joy of giving.

Homes of Hope is one of many ministries and agencies battling global poverty, and the need is enormous. A UN-Habitat report estimates that by 2020 over one billion people will be living in slums with inadequate housing. In light of these dire statistics, it is easy for people to feel fatalistic and give up even trying to make a difference. These numbers produce a kind of paralysis of action because we figure our efforts would be too insignificant to make a meaningful impact. The conclusion becomes, "What does it matter?" While it is true that one person can't change the whole world, it is possible to change one person's whole world.

From the moment I first heard it, I was inspired by the "Star Thrower" story, written by Loren Eisley in 1969. In summary, it tells of a storm that washed many starfish so high up onto the beach that they couldn't make it back into the water. A young boy began throwing the starfish back into the water one at a time. Soon a man walked up and saw what the boy was doing. He looked out at the thousands of starfish stranded on the beach and told the boy he would never be able to get all of them back into the water. "What difference can you possibly make?" The boy picked up another starfish and threw it back into the water. "I made a difference to that one."

The starfish story has spun off into greeting cards, bookmarks, and content for motivational speeches all over the world. I am not sure when or how it found its way into the Homes of Hope movement, but it did and I love it. The belief that it matters to the one has led to the helping of the many.

Jesus says in Matthew 25, "Truly I tell you, whatever you did for one of the least of these brothers and sisters of mine, you did for me." My life has been devoted to searching for ways to effect transformational change for "the least of these." Sam's question helped me define that core calling and why it is so important to me and the organization I lead.

A key question we have to ask ourselves while engaging a broken world is, what exactly do we owe the poor? The answers are not easy because poverty has many dimensions. But there are answers, and there is hope. Typically, when we think about poverty, we measure it primarily in financial terms. Much of the modern view of how to help the poor centers around helping them get access to more money. But money in and of itself will not solve the issue of poverty.

It's worth noting that many successful people, including the most famous person of all, Jesus Christ, grew up in simplicity, without lots of money. Jesus was raised in a loving family that provided him with all the basics: food, water, shelter, health care, clothing, education, and vocation (carpentry). Access to the basics of life are what we owe the poor, but to see real transformation take place in our broken world, we must also address the spiritual and relational brokenness of people.

Sam's poignant question also reminded me that not so long ago I was a starfish lying on the beach and someone took time to pick me up and throw me back into the water. His name was Dale Pederson.

TWO

It Matters to This One

"Never worry about numbers. Help one person at a time and always start with the person nearest you."

Mother Teresa

G R O W I N G up, I never dreamed of starting a global home-building movement for the poor. I was a skinny, six-foot-two, brown-haired, steady-C high school student who played JV basketball and baseball in an unremarkable suburb of Minneapolis. Since I was not talented enough to make the varsity teams, I started working as a bag boy at Penny's Super Market in Fridley, Minnesota. One of my coworkers at Penny's was Dale Pederson, and meeting Dale changed my life.

One day Dale invited me to a youth Bible study at Redeemer Lutheran Church, and I accepted the invitation. That evening we sat on carpet squares in the old chapel as a young Australian pastor named Neil Reichelt read through various parables of Jesus. Then we talked about what they could mean for our lives. I found myself deeply connecting with the messages each story conveyed. Neil's teaching style was interactive, and he asked thought-provoking questions. It wasn't a sermon, but a discussion. I had been raised Catholic, and I attended mass weekly with my family. However, the Bible studies at Redeemer energized me spiritually like nothing I'd ever experienced.

My faith in Christ came alive as I started applying the teachings of Jesus in my everyday life. To me the lessons outlined in the Gospels were no longer simple historic narratives. They taught principles I could apply in my own life's context. Reading the Scriptures for myself created a dramatic shift in the way I related to God. The more I read and absorbed of Jesus and his message, the more my heart and behaviors changed.

Dale picked me up every Wednesday night and drove us to the youth group meetings. A few months into my connection with Redeemer, Neil invited me to be a counselor for their sixth-grade summer camp at Faith Haven located in Battle Lake, Minnesota. My two main assignments would be to make sure these rambunctious sixth graders didn't burn down the dorm and to do a forty-five-minute Bible study with some campers each day. I figured I could handle those responsibilities for a week, and I quickly said yes to the opportunity.

My career as a camp counselor got off to a rough start. I struggled through the Bible study assignment as I had no idea how to teach sixth graders about the Bible. The second night of the camp, Neil asked me to say grace before dinner, and a bolt of panic shot through me. I launched into a long, rambling prayer that Neil had to cut short.

I soon found my stride and came to enjoy praying and teaching the Bible to the young campers. In the afternoons we swam, played basketball, and found other forms of fun. After a few days at camp, my raw leadership gifts started to emerge. Late one night I organized all the boys in my dorm into a race around the flagpole in our underwear. We called our stunt "The Undy 500," and the boys loved it.

Unfortunately, Neil did not. He approached me with a tense smile and said, "Promise me you will never do that again." I assured Neil it was our first and last Undy 500.

Neil may have been unhappy with me in that moment, but the important thing was that he still gave me a chance to serve and took time to mentor me. He was doing what Jesus had done with his dysfunctional crew—he was discipling me.

Over that week, many of the boys began to soften up spiritually, and some confided their problems to me. Just as Dale and Neil had invested in me, now I was investing in others, and I loved it. When it came time for the campers to say good-bye, I was caught off guard by their grateful responses. I was also thankful—especially to Neil for believing in me and modeling good leadership.

As we rode the bus back to Fridley, I thought about what I might do the rest of my life. I wasn't exactly sure what it would be, but I knew it would involve investing in people. Through my experiences with Dale and Neil and the campers, I discovered the joy of serving others. Dale told me years later that he had set a goal to influence one person's life each year, and in 1975 I was that one person. Over the next few years I became a consistent volunteer leader in the youth group. Eventually, I even taught myself how to play the guitar so I could help lead worship.

My church friends and I regularly discussed ways to live out our faith other than just attending church on Sunday. In my junior year of high school, seven of us formed a nonprofit corporation called Soteria so that we could host Christian concerts and do local outreaches. One of the founding members was my close friend Todd Johnson. Todd was two years older than I, and in the fall of 1976 he went off to Montana State University to get his engineering degree.

While in Montana, Todd saw a movie called *Brother Sun, Sister Moon*, which told the story of Saint Francis of Assisi, the son of a wealthy textile merchant who decided to sell all of his possessions and dedicate himself to helping the poor. Saint Francis's story was so inspiring to Todd that when he came home for summer break, we rented the movie and showed it to the youth group. We all were inspired by the movie and began to look for ways to sacrifice what we had in order to serve the Lord.

The Soteria vision kept growing, and Todd thought it would be ideal to have an office and community outreach center. To raise money for it, Todd hosted a giant garage sale dubbed "The Everything Sale" because all of us involved sold almost everything we owned. Toward the end of the day, Todd made one further sacrifice and put his beloved Olin Mark 4 skis up for sale, which helped us reach our goal of $3,000 in one weekend! We never did open a community center, but we used the money to do additional outreaches in our community. We were young and full of zeal.

After graduating from high school, I decided to work for a year and save some money before attending St. John's University. I got a job working as a carpet-layer along with my dad at my uncle Len's carpet shop in downtown Minneapolis. It was during that year that I first heard about YWAM. A neighbor suggested I attend a church service that featured a special missions speaker. The speaker said YWAM was started in 1960 by Loren Cunningham as an interdenominational, international missionary organization that worked with young people. The speaker told stories of God using young people to smuggle Bibles into communist Eastern Europe. As I listened to the speaker's accounts, I started imagining myself doing the same things. The more he spoke, the more excited I got. At the end of the meeting, I hurried to the back table to grab a brochure.

The key words for me were *youth* and *mission*. It was refreshing to find an organization whose main goal was to inspire young people to get involved in the Great Commission of Jesus. Todd had also heard about YWAM. In the fall of 1978, as I headed off to St. John's University to start my freshman year, Todd paused his university career to attend a Discipleship Training School (DTS) in Los Angeles. DTS is YWAM's entry-level program and involves three months of classes centered on the nature and character of God, devotional life, intercession, missions, and relationships. At the end of the classes, students are sent on international outreaches to apply what they have learned.

Todd returned to Minnesota after his YWAM training, and he was bubbling over with stories about his experiences. I was enjoying university, but I was also restless inside. Todd's stories about the wonderful teachings he had heard and his outreach in Mexico sparked a new interest in YWAM. At the end of our weekend together, as we were walking to Todd's car, he said, "Do you know that two and a half *billion* people in the world have never heard of Jesus?"

"Well, everyone has heard of Jesus, but they just don't want to follow, right?" I responded.

"No, they have never even heard his name a single time."

Todd's words stuck in my head. The thought of billions of people never having heard the name of Jesus troubled me. Jesus loved the world so much that he was willing to die on the cross to provide forgiveness and eternal life to all who would call on his name. Of course everyone is free to believe whatever they want, but I thought it was important that everyone around the world hear his message at least one time.

On Monday morning I had an early psychology class in a large auditorium. As I climbed up the center stairs and sat in the back of the class, I was still preoccupied with everything Todd had said to me. As the class started, I couldn't focus on a word the teacher was saying. Suddenly my spirit was alert, and I sensed God was speaking to me. I didn't hear an audible voice, but it may as well have been one. In that moment I felt certain God was calling me to join YWAM and to go immediately.

Up until then I acknowledged that God could speak to people, but I wasn't sure he had ever spoken to me. I thought it would be hard to distinguish God's voice from my own self-talk or good ideas. This definitely wasn't my good idea. At 8:30 a.m. on that Monday morning I suddenly had a conviction that God was speaking to me and calling me to leave everything I knew in Minnesota and join YWAM in Los Angeles.

I wasn't sure how to tell my parents that I was now dropping out of college to be a missionary, nor how they would take the news. The next day I made the seventy-mile drive from St. John's to my parents' home in Fridley. I had the utmost admiration for both my mother and father because they had sacrificed so much for their eight children. My father spent long hours on his knees as a carpet-layer and even took side jobs to earn extra income. My parents and I were close, and I wanted to show them the respect they deserved as I told them of the new plan for my future.

Completing a college degree was important to my parents, and I knew they would be upset when they heard I was leaving St. John's University. I decided to take them out for dinner, knowing that if we were in a public place, they wouldn't yell at me. My stomach was churning as we took our seats at Mr. Steak restaurant. I stalled for as long as possible, but finally I cleared my throat and leaned forward in my chair.

"Mom, Dad, I'm going to quit school and join Youth With A Mission. They have a Discipleship Training School that I want to attend. It's in Los Angeles."

My mom looked at me confused. "Youth with a what?" she asked.

"Youth With A Mission," I repeated.

"Well, what is that?"

I made my best attempt to outline some of the topics and teachers that were a part of the school that Todd had told me about, but the truth was I did not know all that much about YWAM. I was basing this huge life-changing decision on an encounter I had with God in the back of my psychology class and Todd's recommendations. I soon found myself running out of words.

"And what are they going to pay you?" my dad interrupted.

"There is no pay involved. I have to raise my own support."

"Okay." He paused and then added, "So, who is going to support you?"

"I believe if God is going to call me to do this, then he will provide," I said.

I tried to sound confident, but I was flooded with an uneasy mix of both fear and faith. My parents had made it clear to me and my siblings that they would support us financially if we were enrolled in school, but once we stopped our studies, their support would end. I had a strong sense that God was leading me to join YWAM despite all of the unknowns. My mom and dad continued to ask questions, but I knew little about the specifics of the enrollment process at YWAM or even all the costs. I wasn't even sure how I was going to make the two-thousand-mile journey to Los Angeles. All I had was faith that God was leading me to go and a belief that he would provide. Eventually my parents understood there was no point in trying to change my mind.

To clear my St. John's tuition bill, I arranged my own "Everything Sale" on the fourth floor of my dorm. I sold most of my possessions, including a nice stereo system, an expensive Olympus OM1 camera, and a bunch of sports equipment. After the sale I was still short of what I needed to pay off my tuition bill. On Friday morning I walked to my student mailbox for the last time. In my mailbox I found an envelope with offering money from my college friends who had heard about what I was doing and wanted to support me. It was my first miracle, and it touched my heart that they were willing to support me to go off to YWAM. The offering money combined with the funds from my dorm sale was enough to pay my full tuition bill, and I walked out of the administration office with a grand total of one dollar left over.

A dollar wasn't going to get me from Minneapolis to Los Angeles, but I was now debt free. To get my travel money, I decided to sell my most precious possession: a beautiful red-wine Ovation guitar with pearl inlays. I had wanted to take it with me to Los Angeles, but I was willing to make any sacrifice necessary to obey what I knew to be God's will.

Saturday morning, my mom drove me to the Greyhound bus station at 6:00 a.m. She gave me a big hug and told me she loved me. A lot had happened in the previous five days, and riding on a bus for the next forty-five hours would give me time to reflect on it all. What would await me in California? I would need God to continue providing if my dream to serve the Lord through YWAM was going to work. As the hours on the bus ticked by, I thought about Saint Francis of Assisi and how he had sold everything he had and went off to serve the poor. And though I didn't know it at the time, I too was on my way to serve the poor.

California, here I come.

THREE

God Will Make a Way

> "Faith is deliberate confidence in the character of God whose ways you may not understand at the time."
>
> *Oswald Chambers*

FROM the moment I arrived at YWAM Los Angeles, I felt perfectly at home. I was surrounded by other students and staff with a similar passion for God.

My small-group leader was an Australian guy named Peter Warren, and right away I loved his quick wit and deep spirituality. He led our daily worship times and often included other staff to join him. One of those helpers was an attractive young woman named Janet Izzett.

One morning Peter introduced me to her and added, "Sean is my most difficult student."

I responded to his jab, saying, "Yeah, I've had to get extra counseling to fix all the problems Peter is creating in my life." Janet smiled and then walked away to meet some of the other students.

Each week in DTS we had a different teacher who spoke on a new topic. They were all great, but my favorite was Dean Sherman. He spoke to us in the morning about relationships and at night about spiritual warfare. Dean would say over and over, "Every problem in the world is a problem of relationships." Our class had a strong sense of community, one in which people interacted with each other and shared about their personal lives at a deep level.

At one of our lectures, YWAM Los Angeles director John Dawson taught about "Our Missionary Calling." "What is your motivation for serving God?" he asked the class. "Is it to please people, or to please God?" Toward the end of his message, John paused and looked out at everyone seated. "I challenge you to ask God to share his heart for the world with you. Go back to your rooms tonight; pray and ask God to fill you with his love for the world. Having God's perspective will be what sustains you in your missionary calling."

John bowed his head and shifted from speaking to us to praying for us as a class. When I opened my eyes after his prayer, I observed him slipping out of the room without lingering to talk to anyone. It felt like a holy moment, so I headed back to my dorm to pray. It started with me pacing awkwardly back and forth on the worn-out carpet next to my bed. I wasn't sure how to ask God for his heart for the world, so I kept repeating, "God, give me your heart for the world. God, give me your heart for the world . . ." Before I knew it, I felt the Spirit of God touching me. I was overwhelmed with emotion and fell face down on the floor. I began crying uncontrollably. This was very unusual considering my Catholic and Lutheran roots and my usual lack of emotion. As I prayed, I felt God's Spirit connect with mine like I had in my psychology class at St. John's just a few weeks before.

I was getting a fresh download from the Holy Spirit of how much God loved the world he had created. It was not an audible voice, but in my spirit I heard the words, "I love the world so much, but who will go, who will go?" I knew I had to respond, and I blurted out, "God, you can use me. Here I am, send me." When I got back on my feet, I opened my eyes and looked around my small dorm room with a sense of wonder at all that had just happened. God had indeed shared his heart with me. I had a deep sense of peace that he had accepted my offer to serve him as a full-time missionary.

During the lecture phase of the school, we were told that our two-month field outreach would to go to San Quintín, in northern Mexico, to work at an orphanage. In June 1979 twenty-five staff and students piled into an old school bus that desperately needed a new paint job and some upholstery work, and four hours later we crossed into Mexico. I immediately noticed a drastic change in the living conditions. Off the paved main road near Tijuana were mostly shanty houses built with scrap wood and tarps. They looked more like the forts my boyhood friends and I had built in the woods of Minnesota. These shacks stood in stark contrast to the opulence and beauty of San Diego, just a few miles away.

How can people live like this? I wondered. *How could they possibly be happy in such a place?*

To my surprise, the Mexican people we met in the Baja desert region seemed remarkably happy. Despite their poverty, they were exceedingly friendly and possessed a strong sense of family and community. They had a contentment about what they possessed, and never seemed to let what they *didn't* have distract them. Our group was met with smiling faces and hugs from the children wherever we went.

I graduated from Discipleship Training School that August, and the experience was everything I had thought it would be and more. I had grown so much in my knowledge and love of God. Peter Warren invited me to attend a second YWAM missions school, and I jumped at the chance. He also mentioned a new work-study option in which I could work a part-time job to earn money for school while attending classes each day. Along with two other classmates, I worked as a caregiver at a nearby mental institution. We worked the night shift from 11:00 p.m. to 7:00 a.m., attended classes all morning, then got some sleep in the afternoon.

This school would also have an international field assignment. One team would go to Thailand to work with Cambodian refugees, and another would go to Australia. I decided to join the Australia team, but a stop at the local grocery store soon squelched my fantasy about hanging out on the beaches there. While standing in the checkout line, the cover of *Time* magazine caught my eye. It had a striking photograph of a mother holding a malnourished baby in her arms. The headline read, "Starvation: Deathwatch in Cambodia." The story inside reported on the crisis of the Cambodian people. Hundreds of thousands were fleeing their country to escape the Pol Pot regime and his vicious Khmer

Rouge soldiers. Most were fleeing to refugee camps in Thailand. I wondered now if God could better use me to serve the refugees in Thailand.

I was still learning about hearing God's voice and was discovering that just putting God's name on a decision didn't mean it was what God wanted. In the DTS we received great teaching on how to hear the voice of God from John's mother, Joy Dawson. One of the key principles taught was "dying to your own ideas, imaginations, and desires." It was vital to make room in your mind and heart for God to speak to you what he wanted. I was beginning to realize that my desire to see the beaches of Australia may have gotten in the way of hearing God's voice correctly.

To get more clarity, I sat down with a notebook to organize all my thoughts and impressions from the Lord. In writing things down, it became abundantly clear that my motives to go to Australia were primarily touristic in nature. With Thailand it was different. God's call to go and help the Cambodian refugees was coming through loud and clear. When I chose to go to Thailand, a deep and abiding peace came over me. It was exactly where I needed to be.

Just before Thanksgiving, Western Airlines had a sale, and I was able to buy a cheap ticket from Los Angeles to Minneapolis. Going home allowed me to connect with some old and new supporters. When I arrived back at my parents' home, I told them I was going to Thailand to work with Cambodian refugees. They seemed proud of me. The plight of the Cambodian people was in the news almost every day.

While in Minnesota, I received wonderful support from family and friends. I returned to LA with enough money to cover my own outreach costs and an additional $800 that I gave to other students who needed help with their airfare and ground fees. John Dawson often said to us, "If you're going to live by faith, you have to give like crazy." That was exactly what I was doing.

On Christmas Day 1979 we landed in Thailand to work with Cambodian refugees settled in camps along the Thailand-Cambodia border. After a few days' rest, our team traveled north to a large World Vision refugee camp. YWAM had established a good working relationship with World Vision, which operated several large camps that were well organized but stark and utilitarian. Simple huts constructed with bamboo poles and thatch roofs were everywhere; only a few of the structures had walls. The refugees had fled for their lives, and many were sick and malnourished. Looking at the picture on the cover of *Time* magazine was one thing, but standing in a refugee camp surrounded by all the heartbreak and human need was overwhelming. These camps provided temporary relief for the refugees, but most of the people did not know if they would ever to return to their homeland or see their relatives again.

In one of the World Vision camps, we entertained the refugees with music and puppet shows. Our shows were a diversion from their lives of boredom and misery, and they also gave us an opportunity to show Christ's love. I suddenly found myself playing guitar in front of crowds as large as two thousand people. I may have been a hack musician back home in Minnesota, but in the refugee camps I was a rock star!

By January 1980 YWAM had hundreds of volunteers serving in refugee camps in Thailand. Many of our staff were given significant leadership responsibilities in the camps because officials could see our love for the people and our willingness to serve and do anything that was needed. We were making God known with a two-handed approach. With one hand we served the practical needs of people, and with the other hand we served their spiritual needs.

While in the transit camps, I was privileged to pray with sixteen Khmer Rouge soldiers after our small team presented a message about the cross of Christ and forgiveness. It was easy to see that the former soldiers were hurting inside because they had committed unspeakable acts of violence and terror at the direction of the dictator Pol Pot. These former soldiers desperately needed change from the inside out, and that change was not going to come from just humanitarian relief. There were lots of tears and prayers that day. Over the next few weeks, we taught them from the Bible what it meant to love God with all their heart and also to love their neighbor as themselves.

I wanted to stay in Thailand, but the YWAM leadership there said I needed to raise a minimum of $350 per month in committed support to be on staff. I had nothing near that amount. When I returned to Southern California, I informed the leadership that I wanted to join YWAM Los Angeles as a full-time staff member. They said they would pray about it while I returned to Minnesota to see what support I could raise. I was living in my parents' basement when I got a phone call from one of the leaders. I sat in stunned silence as he said he didn't think it was a good idea for me to join their staff and suggested I consider other options. I had gambled everything I had on becoming a missionary with YWAM. It was like someone punched me in the gut. My dream was dead in the water.

I was depressed for days after that call. The opportunity to go back to Thailand had closed, and now a return to Los Angeles was closed too. I decided I would find a job, save up some money, and then look for an opportunity to rejoin YWAM later. I went back to work at my uncle's carpet business, I reengaged with the youth group at Redeemer Lutheran Church, and I moved into a rental house with a bunch of other guys from the church.

After nine months of working in Minnesota, something totally unexpected happened. Our Soteria group invited John Dawson to meet with us, and to our surprise he agreed to come. Ten of us attended a late-November retreat at a lake cabin about an hour from Fridley. When we arrived, a light dusting of snow covered the ground and the edges of the lake were frozen solid. At one point during the weekend, John took me aside to talk. I told him my full story of leaving St. John's University, my encounter with God in the dorm room after hearing the message on "Our Missionary Calling," and my experiences in Thailand. He was surprised I hadn't stayed on at YWAM Los Angeles. Apparently he was unaware I'd been told not to return.

John possessed an uncanny ability for assessing a person's talents and potential. He saw me in that moment, not for what I was then, but for the person I would become. "God has a call on your life, and I want you to return to YWAM Los Angeles to pursue it," he said.

My joy was so great that I could barely answer. "Okay, yes . . . I will. Thank you, John. I'll come as soon as I can arrange it."

Saying I couldn't leave town fast enough would be an understatement. Before sunrise the day after Christmas in 1980, I left Minnesota in a $400 rusted-out Oldsmobile Cutlass, towing my motorcycle behind on a small trailer. My adrenaline was pumping so strongly that I drove from Minnesota to New Mexico, a total of twenty-three hours, without stopping to rest.

One blessing of returning to Los Angeles was reconnecting with Janet Izzett, who was working as a secretary for Joy Dawson. Over the next few weeks I found myself frequently hanging out at the big YWAM house in Sunland, California, where Janet and other staff women lived. Janet had sparkling green eyes and an amazing smile. Her close friends called her *flaca*, the Spanish word for "skinny." At first I was much more interested in her than she was in me. I was two years younger. Although I had grown more mature since my DTS, I still had a playful, goofy side that she endured more than enjoyed.

One night after watching a movie with Janet and other friends at the Sunland house, I thundered out of the parking lot on my big Honda 750 motorcycle. It had a black windjammer complete with a cassette tape stereo sound system, and I felt like I was Mr. Cool each time I rode it. As I accelerated on a curvy road near Sunland Park, I realized I was going too fast. I hit my brakes in a panic and slammed right into a curb. The impact shot me off the bike like a rocket, and I hit the curb on my right side just below my rib cage. I rolled a few feet and then stood up, thinking I was okay. Then pain shot through my stomach, and I collapsed in the dirt. For several minutes I lay there writhing. My bike was still in the street, the motor running and music blasting. Eventually, a car slowed down and the driver shouted out, "Do you need some help?"

"Yes, please call an ambulance."

I was taken to a small hospital in Lake View Terrace, about fifteen minutes away. The attending nurse was initially convinced I had nothing more than bruised ribs. I was so thankful when Janet came walking into the room. I found myself reaching out to grab her hand. About then a nurse took my blood pressure and sounded the alarm when she barely found a reading. The hospital staff started scrambling and rushed me into surgery. They knew what I did not: I was experiencing massive internal bleeding and would die soon if they could not stop it.

I awoke the next day in a hospital bed. I had a ventilation machine helping me breathe, a catheter, and a twelve-inch-long incision running from the top center of my rib cage straight down to the bottom of my stomach. I also had two drainage tubes inserted into me on the right and left sides of my stomach. I was told that the doctors had to remove my right kidney, which had shattered when I hit the curb.

I was relieved to know I could still live a full life with only one kidney. Over the next twenty-four hours my mood brightened, especially when Janet and a few other friends came to visit. Janet visited me regularly in the hospital. She was so easy to talk to, and the more we talked, the more we realized that our values and calling to serve God were much the same.

After the first week I said to her, "You know, it's almost worth losing a kidney to have you come and visit me every day."

"Well, I enjoy our visits. And besides, someone has to check in on you to keep you out of trouble." She flashed that beautiful smile again.

After ten days in the hospital, I was released and told by the doctors I had to rest for the next six weeks while my stomach muscles healed. My parents offered to fly me home, but John Dawson encouraged me to stay in LA. During those six weeks I spent most of my free time thinking up creative ways to hang out with Janet.

One day over coffee I asked her how she had decided to join YWAM.

"It was something John Dawson said at a youth service I attended. He challenged us, saying, 'If you have always wanted to do something great for God, now is the time.' I was attending Portland State University at the time and decided right then I was going to put my university education on hold and attend a YWAM training school."

"Wow, that's similar to my story, being in university and sensing a call from God to quit school to join YWAM."

"If you want to know the real truth," Janet said, "my call to missions came much earlier, through a puppet show at a summer camp when I was ten years old."

"A puppet show! We used puppets in Thailand with the refugees. They loved them."

Our first official date as a couple was Valentine's Day 1981. Since I didn't have money to take her out to dinner, I decided to cook a homemade pizza for her in the guys' dorm house. Janet and I had known each other as friends for about two years, but over the course of those six weeks I fell deeply in love with her. I knew Janet liked me, but she didn't let fleeting emotions guide her. She considered marriage one of life's most important decisions, and she wanted to get it right. I wanted to marry her and decided to escalate my own prayer times about the subject to get some additional confirmation from the Lord.

A few days after committing to pray more about our future together, I woke up at 2:00 a.m. totally alert. A random Bible reference stuck in my head—Proverbs 18:22. I wanted to know what that verse said, so I slipped into the bathroom with my Bible and turned on the light. The verse said, "He who finds a wife finds what is good and receives favor from the LORD." This Bible verse, along with the amazing way it came to me, was additional confirmation that Janet was the right one for me. A few weeks later we had another serious talk, and Janet said she felt peace that we were to marry. In Janet, I knew I had found the perfect life partner. She had the same life calling and was willing to live by faith and obey God no matter the cost.

In March we drove up to Healdsburg, a small Northern California town where Janet's parents lived. Her family of eight had moved often when Janet was growing up, typically living in small rental homes. She told me there were many winters when her dad, Al, struggled to find the seasonal work that sustained them. The struggle to survive was ingrained in Janet at an early age, but so was a dependence on God, who provided in miraculous ways throughout her childhood.

As Janet and I sat on the couch in her parents' living room, Al came out of his bedroom and stood in the hallway looking me over. After a few tense moments, I found the nerve to ask, "Mr. Izzett, may I have permission to marry your daughter?"

With a wry smile he answered, "Yes, and I will give you $500 and a ladder." With that, he went back into his room. While I was relieved that he had said yes, I was confused about what a ladder had to do with getting married. Janet explain to me that he was joking. The ladder was for me to get up to her bedroom window so we could elope.

After arriving back in Los Angeles from Healdsburg, we went to a pay phone and called my mom and dad to tell them the good news. My mom got on the phone first, and her reaction wasn't the joyous response I'd hoped for. "How can you get married with no money? How are you going to support her? What about health insurance? What will you do if you have children? How will you support them?" I valued my mom's approval, and these were legitimate concerns that I had no immediate answers for. I hung up the phone a bit stunned as doubt and fear started to creep into my mind. Janet had a good home church that regularly supported her, but I was living on random gifts from friends. I owed the bank some money for my motorcycle and also owed Lake

View Terrace Hospital $3,500. I had health insurance, but the remaining balance was a co-pay that I was responsible for. We had no money to buy rings or pay for other wedding expenses.

When I told Janet about my mother's reaction to our wedding plans, she could see I was shaken. She took my hand in hers, and we started to pray. Instantly, I felt the peace of God come over me. As Janet prayed, a strong impression from the Lord came into my mind. I knew it was him speaking to my spirit. What I heard was, *I have taken care of you as a single person and Janet as a single person, and I will take care of you both together and all your kids. Don't fear and don't be afraid. I am with you.*

The clarity and speed of God speaking to me, combined with a wave of peace coming over me, lifted the disappointment right out of me. I started to laugh with relief. Since Janet was still praying aloud, she was annoyed with my outburst of laughter until I explained what had just happened. This word from the Lord was for us and for our future children. We had both learned to trust God as single people, and now God was showing us that we could trust him as a married couple and eventually as a family.

As the weeks passed there were no immediate financial breakthroughs. The stress of future wedding expenses, combined with the bank loan and hospital bill, was starting to wear on me. I found a cassette tape in the YWAM library of one of Joy Dawson's messages, entitled "God Will Make a Way." The title intrigued me, and I listened to the entire teaching. At the end Joy said to take the time to hear from God specifically as to what to do next.

In response to the teaching, I found a quiet spot to pray. I gave God all my medical bills, my motorcycle debt, and our wedding expenses. I bowed my head and waited on God in silence, not exactly sure what would happen next. After several moments of silence, an impression from the Lord popped into my mind: *Go to the hospital. Go today, go now!*

It was already mid-afternoon, and the hospital was thirty minutes away. I drove straight to Lake View Terrace Hospital. Inside, I went down several hallways to the small financial office. I was escorted to a small cubicle and sat across from a caseworker assigned to my account. I informed the woman I wanted to pay my bill, but I had no money.

"Is there a scholarship fund I could apply to?" I asked.

"I'm sorry, there isn't. You are going to have to pay your bill."

I was about to start questioning my guidance from the Lord when her expression brightened. "There's a special medical aid program for needy residents of California. Have you heard of it?"

"No, I only moved here a few months ago, and I'm not sure I qualify as a resident yet."

"You became a qualified resident on the first day you moved into California."

She continued to look into my file, sorting through all the pages. With a bit of shock and enthusiasm, she looked up and smiled. "You know what? It's a good thing you came in today because this is the last day you can apply for help from this program. Your eligibility expires tomorrow."

I had a hard time believing what she said. After filling out the paperwork, the entire balance for my medical expenses was paid in full! I was so glad I took the time to listen to the Lord and get the details about what to do next. A few days later I sold my motorcycle. I had no intention of ever riding that thing again. It had almost taken my life, and I didn't want to offer up any more chances.

The breakthroughs kept coming. To our great surprise, Janet's sister, Pam, called and told us she was sending us some money, which was enough to buy wedding rings. Janet's parents came through with the $500 her dad had promised. Janet was able to borrow a friend's wedding dress, and my parents gave us $500 to help with the wedding.

Our simple but lovely wedding ceremony was held on June 13, 1981. For our honeymoon, Jim and Joy Dawson gifted us the use of their trailer, located in the mountains near Wrightwood, California. We drove off in my rusty Oldsmobile with streamers and tin cans in tow. To start our new life together we had little money and no place of our own to live, but we had each other and the promise of God about our future.

FOUR

Servant Leadership

"Everyone can be great because everyone can serve."

Martin Luther King Jr.

A YEAR after our wedding, Janet and I attended a conference at Twin Oaks Ranch in Texas. One morning I found a nice spot next to a small lake to sit and have my devotions. In my daily reading I came across a teaching by Jesus about servant leadership. I read, "You know that the rulers of the Gentiles lord it over them, and their high officials exercise authority over them. Not so with you. Instead, whoever wants to become great among you must be your servant, and whoever wants to be first must be your slave—just as the Son of Man did not come to be served, but to serve, and to give his life as a ransom for many" (Matthew 20:25–28).

A few chapters later I read more of what Jesus had to say about servant leadership. "The greatest among you will be your servant. For those who exalt themselves will be humbled, and those who humble themselves will be exalted" (Matthew 23:11–12).

As I reflected on these teachings, I felt a disconnect. How could someone be a servant *and* a leader at the same time? The concept of

29

finding greatness through serving didn't make sense to me. I felt called
to leadership, but in my way of thinking, leaders were supposed to be in
charge of things and tell everyone else what to do. How could someone
change the world as just a servant?

There by the lake in Texas, I sensed God was asking me to humble
myself and embrace a fresh vision for my life, one of being a servant
leader. Although I lacked full understanding, I decided that if Jesus was
a servant leader, then I would strive to be one too.

Later that day I approached John Dawson and asked if we could
talk. I told John what God had spoken to me. "I am not sure what to
do next, but I'm called to be a servant leader. I want you to know I am
willing to serve YWAM Los Angeles wherever the need is greatest." John
smiled back at me. I thought he would be so impressed by my humble
attitude that he would ask me to run the next school or take on some
other important ministry role. To my surprise he said, "We need you in
the print shop."

The print shop? What did I know about printing? Plus, I could
barely spell! But after a thoughtful pause I said, "Okay, I am willing to
serve in the print shop."

Once back in Los Angeles I discovered that my new job entailed
identifying fresh stories to include in the YWAM Los Angeles monthly
newsletter, typesetting the text, then printing the newsletter on an old
AB Dick 360 press. When that was done, I assembled all the letters into
envelopes, sorted them by zip code, and mailed them out.

Working in the print shop taught me many valuable lessons, especially about the power of communication. These mailings to donors,
potential students, churches, and other friends of YWAM Los Angeles
were vital to the ministry. Working in the print shop allowed me to
serve a vision bigger than my own. It broke me of the need to impose
my agenda on others, and as a result I became a better listener.

As my season of service in the print shop came to a close, Janet and
I found ourselves again working with the Discipleship Training Schools.
By 1985 Janet and I were senior leaders in the training department,
but we sensed God's Spirit was nudging us in a new direction. In 1984
our founder, Loren Cunningham, wrote a book about the beginnings
of YWAM entitled *Is That Really You, God?* When Loren was starting

YWAM, God gave him a vision of waves of young people going out into all the world.

As I read Loren's book, something sparked in my spirit. Janet and I were now part of those waves of young people, and we were so grateful. YWAM had become known globally as the leader in short-term mission trips, but at our LA training center, our short-term numbers were almost nonexistent. I thought, *What if we put together outreach opportunities for teens?*

Inspired by what we sensed was God's next assignment for us, Janet and I started to mobilize youth for short-term mission trips during their spring and summer school breaks. We worked hard to get the word out through mailings and phone calls to youth groups. We set an initial goal to see six hundred youth go out each year, but the next year only thirty youth came to our outreach at the World Cup soccer matches in Mexico City.

After that outreach, John Dawson and I flew to Brazil for some meetings. One night I couldn't sleep, so I went for a walk out on a large soccer field. Under a dazzling star-filled sky, I felt God's Spirit speaking to me again, not in an audible voice, but in a gentle nudge in the form of a question: "Will you believe me for a thousand youth a year?" Without any idea of how that could happen, I said, "Yes." Immediately, I started praying for a thousand youth to join our outreaches. It was a short transactional moment with the Lord, but it gave me a sense of confirmation that we were on the right track.

The next year we organized some great trips—one went around the world, another was a bike outreach to Europe, others were to exotic places like the Amazon—but only eighty young people responded. Often youth would sign up for a trip only to cancel a few weeks later.

A breakthrough moment happened for us when I received a call from my brother-in-law, Charlie Morales, who was a youth pastor from Oregon. He said, "Sean, I like your ideas for short-term youth outreaches, but your trips are all designed for individuals and are too long and expensive for my youth group. Could you and Janet design a trip for next summer that would work for forty kids from our church?" Simply put, Charlie was saying that our present outreach design didn't fit his church's group needs. I began to wonder, was this what God had wanted all along—for me to serve groups, not individuals? Had I drifted from a servant leadership posture and imposed my own agenda on the vision God had given me? My one previous experience working with a church youth group had been a disastrous Mexico outreach in which we drove too far, everyone got sick, and we ran out of money and barely made it home.

Charlie's call reignited the idea of group-based trips. Perhaps serving whole churches rather than individuals was the key to achieving my God-given goal of a thousand youth a year. Charlie liked the idea of going to Mexico as long as he and his group didn't have to pay for a plane ticket. Tijuana crossed my mind as a possible outreach location since it was only three hours' drive south of Los Angeles.

By the late 1980s, Tijuana was no longer a sleepy little border town. It had some nine hundred foreign factories and a robust trading and tourist economy. Located in the Mexican state of Baja California, or *Baja Norte*, it had become a magnet for those looking for jobs and a better life. An average of five thousand people every month were moving into the area from all over Mexico and Central America. Sadly, many of the new arrivals struggled to survive in garage-sized shelters made with cast-off building materials found at the dump or at secondhand lumber yards. Wages in the factories were so low that it was virtually impossible for workers to feed their families, keep their kids in school, buy a few clothes, travel to work, and have enough left over for housing. It was a challenging life at best.

I mentioned our desire to take a team to Tijuana to some friends who frequently traveled there. They gave me some local contacts, one of whom was Sergio Gomez. Sergio was a burly former boxer with a shiny gold front tooth. I liked him right away, and after a few weeks I learned more of his story. As a boy, he got caught up in gangs and violence. He was in and out of jail until miraculously, at the age of fourteen, he was able to get a job and leave his gang life. By sixteen he had opened his heart to the Lord and was a changed person. Times were tough for Sergio, and he ended up homeless. As he got older, he trained to be a pastor and even started an orphanage. Along the way he began building homes for the poor because he knew what it was like not to have one.

Sergio couldn't have been more gracious in helping me organize a trip for Charlie's youth group. He even found accommodations for us at a Bible school that was out of session for the summer. So Janet and I led Charlie and his forty kids to Tijuana. In the mornings we had worship and teaching. Then we all headed to the orphanage to serve and participate in children's programs at local churches. Overall, the trip was a great success.

Sergio had opened my eyes and heart to the city of Tijuana with its great needs and opportunities. Over the next year, Janet and I shifted away from mobilizing individuals and worked to get more groups to come to Tijuana. My relationship with Sergio grew as I embraced his vision of serving the city, and particularly his heart and passion for the poor. His energy was contagious. I wasn't sure when he slept as he had so many ministry initiatives. Sergio began including me in monthly pastors' alliance meetings and introduced me to orphanage directors, as well as some city officials. Because we were getting more calls from groups wanting mission trips, I welcomed his help and connections.

On one of my visits, Sergio drove me around in his orange GMC pickup. The truck must have had 150,000 miles on it, and every inch was covered with dust. Sergio gave me a guided tour of eastern Tijuana, known as El Florido, where thousands of Tijuana's new arrivals were crammed into canyons and steep, dusty hillsides known as *colonias*. This is where Sergio was building what he called *Casas de Amor* (Homes of Love). As we drove on, I observed tremendous need. Large families were living under blue tarps or old garage doors lashed together into a roof.

"Why would people live like this?" I asked Sergio.

"They are smart," he replied.

"Smart? How so?"

"Most of these families have jobs and can afford a small apartment in the city. But they know once they pay their rent, that money is gone forever. Here, they can buy some land so they will have something to pass on to their children."

I sat in silence, trying to absorb what Sergio was telling me.

"Sean, you see poor people, but I see fighters," he continued. "I see committed families working hard for a better life. These are the people I am called to help." I could hear the emotion rising in Sergio's voice.

"What about helping the poor who don't have any land? What about them?" I asked.

"Being honest," Sergio said, glancing over at me from behind the wheel, "I have learned to focus on only helping those who show some initiative to help themselves. So I wait to see who will buy land and then help those families."

I was beginning to grasp Sergio's approach to helping the poor.

"Don't get me wrong, Sean. I will give some food and other small supplies to a family that is truly in need, but I have learned to only build my Casas de Amor for those who have first made the sacrifice to buy their own land."

Sergio's insights were intriguing, and we continued to ride together in silence as he navigated the bumpy dirt roads of El Florido. I looked out the window as we drove past hundreds of makeshift one-room shacks with dirt floors. "What happens when it rains?" I asked, already starting to consider how awful it must be for people living on the hills.

"Sean, you have no idea how bad it is for these families. It's hard to even drive my four-wheel-drive truck out here. It's truly miserable, and most of the roofing is so bad that everything a family owns gets wet."

"Why don't they just build a better house?"

Sergio turned slowly and looked at me as if I were a five-year-old. "You don't understand Mexico, do you? These people are making less than $75 a week. Almost half of that money goes to pay for the land they are paying down. The rest goes to getting to work, feeding their families, and buying clothes. There is no money left over to buy building materials. Only after they get their land paid for can they then start investing in a real house."

"How long does it take for them to pay for the land?"

"Typically, seven to ten years."

It was difficult to wrap my head around the fact that the poor Mexican families had to live in such conditions for that amount of time. In response to my silence, Sergio glanced over at me again. "Now you know why I build Casas de Amor." He tapped his chest with his right hand. "I know what it's like to be a kid without a good home to live in. I lived in my car for two years. Then God changed my life when I was a teenager and filled my heart with love for people. I do what I do because God first loved me and now I love people."

Sergio leaned into the steering wheel and turned us onto another dirt road that was even bumpier than the last. Together we swayed back and forth in our seats.

"Sean, let me tell you a story," he said with a smile exposing his big gold front tooth. "Years ago, I built a house for a man whose family needed help. They had land, but they had horrible shelter and were suffering. The husband had a drug problem and was very selfish. The wife was most likely staying in the marriage for the benefit of the kids. As we finished building the house and handed the keys to them at the dedication, the husband came up to me weeping because God had touched his life."

"What do you mean?" I asked.

"You won't believe it. The man came to me and said, 'I don't even know this group that is building my house, but they care about my family more than I do.'"

"Wow," I said. "That's a powerful revelation of what God's love is all about."

"The story gets better," Sergio replied, now grinning from ear to ear. "He is now drug-free and a pastor of a small church."

I couldn't help but smile too. "Does every family have something like that happen after the house build?"

Sergio thought for a moment, carefully choosing his words. "Every family gets a revelation of the love of God, but each has a different reaction to what they receive," he said. "You can't judge the effect a home has on a family after just a few weeks or months, because the real impact is on the next generation—their kids and their grandkids."

Sergio had become an important mentor in my life. During our ride together he taught me not only how to understand the poverty of El Florido but how to serve the poor. He explained that he built simple houses, but most families would add onto them later. Since most sheeting and drywall came in four-foot-wide pieces, Sergio's houses were sixteen feet by twenty feet, creating maximum efficiency and a good bang for the buck. Each house had three windows, a door, two small eight-by-ten-foot bedrooms, and a larger kitchen/dining area.

The homes were funded by whatever group came to build with him and were given free of charge to families that met Sergio's criteria. The method Sergio used to determine who to help was simple but powerful.

"The most important factor is that they own the land on which the house will be built. The next factor is whether they have children," he explained. "I also consider their income level, and I always do a site visit to see if the family truly needs a home."

I loved that Sergio never considered himself superior to the families he was helping. He recognized they were all made in the image of God, just as I had discovered in my work with refugees in Thailand years before. The bottom line was that these people needed help, and we both believed we were called to help them. I sensed something special was about happen in Tijuana.

FIVE

An Offering to Jesus

"For it is in giving that we receive."

Francis of Assisi

OVER the next few years, our numbers increased from a maximum of eighty participants a year using the individual model to six hundred a year using the group-based model. The more trips we arranged, the stronger the connection became between YWAM Los Angeles and the city of Tijuana. I hit the road regularly, commuting back and forth to Mexico with teams, then heading north to recruit more church youth groups.

We soon outgrew the little Bible school we were renting to host teams in the summer. In December 1989, Sergio helped us find our own six-thousand-square-foot outreach building located in the Playas (beach) section of Tijuana. The building was only three blocks from the US border fence and right across the street from the Pacific Ocean. A weathered lighthouse stood at the end of the street, and our property backed up against a large bullring stadium. Overall, it felt like a safe place for teams to stay, but the building was in rough shape. It had no showers, kitchen, or walls. To make matters worse, there was garbage everywhere. Still, I was partial to the property from the moment I laid eyes on it. The rent was cheap, and I felt that, once renovated, it would be an ideal residence for youth teams visiting Baja.

I have always been a dreamer and visionary, and often when other people see problems, I see opportunities. Fortunately, Janet provides a good balance to this tendency to dream too much. She has the patience to let me process ideas and gives me space and time to discover God's purposes. Janet knew we would go somewhere only when we both were sure God was directing us.

Because of our increasing outreach numbers, we began to discuss whether we should move to Mexico. The Playas property needed lots of work, but we had little money to execute renovations. Like the people of El Florido, we scrounged for discarded or used appliances, furniture, and building materials. One afternoon I spotted a twelve-foot roll of black felt on the side of the road. I stopped and dragged the roll to my van. Since we didn't have the money for drywall, we used the black felt to separate the girls' and the guys' sections of our building. We eventually fixed the bathrooms, but we still had no showers. We rented rooms at a nearby hotel, and everybody would take turns going there to shower.

In January 1990 we convened our first YWAM Los Angeles staff meeting of the new decade. After dropping off our two children at school and preschool, Janet took a seat next to me in the room. Our director, Dave Gustaveson, stood up and addressed the staff. "I was out on a prayer walk recently, and I felt the Lord speak something unique to my heart. He said that in two weeks' time we were to have a special offering for Jesus."

The room got quiet. This concept didn't make sense to me. An offering for Jesus? How would we get the money to him once we had collected it? I raised my hand. "Dave, don't you think it would be better if we decided what the offering was for before we collect it?"

"No," Dave told me. "That's not how this process is going to work. I want our staff and students to think and pray about what amount they are giving. Then they should imagine they are putting those funds into the hands of Jesus to be used for whatever he wants."

Each of us had taken part in many offerings in YWAM, but none like this one. Two weeks later, with fifty staff present, we took an offering of $2,000. Not bad coming from a bunch of missionaries dependent on God for their provision! Dave formed a small committee to decide what to do with the money and asked me to join. We were all eager to put the money to good use. After several meetings we still couldn't agree on what to do. We discussed options such as dispersing the funds to the homeless shelters in Hollywood or to refugee camps in Thailand. While in Tijuana on one of my trips, it dawned on me that this money could be used to build a home for a needy family. Jesus would certainly give his offering to help the poor! From the moment I pitched the idea to the other leaders in Los Angeles, it resonated with everyone. The idea of having a two-day project that we could all participate in—one that would change a family's life—was compelling.

I contacted Sergio, who was more than happy to find a family in need and help acquire the tools and materials our group would need to build a house. The money may have come from YWAM Los Angeles, but Sergio was supplying the vision and heart for the project. In May 1990 eighteen staff drove to Tijuana to build a single house for a needy Mexican family. We all raised additional funds to cover our transportation, housing, and food. I was excited to participate but had no vision or goal to do more than one home.

As providence would have it, on this trip I took my daughter, Andrea, who was three years old at the time. Janet was reluctant to send her along, but fortunately one of the staff women agreed to help me keep an eye on her.

We would be building in El Florido for a family of five that Sergio selected. We arrived at the work site on Saturday morning to find a sixteen-by-twenty concrete slab, a pile of wood, and other building materials. Our group formed a circle and, with the help of a translator, introduced ourselves to the family members who were living in a scrap-wood shack behind the build site. The father told us he worked as a day laborer in construction, and his wife cleaned houses when she could find the work. We then prayed together, asking God to bless the family and the house build. Sergio got us going in different teams, building the walls, trusses, and painting the siding. The family joyfully worked alongside us.

Later in the day I asked the mother if I could see where they were living, and she took me inside. I was stunned by what I saw. It was one small room with a tarp for a roof, no windows, and a dirt floor. It had a single bed, a tiny broken-down stove, and piles of clothes. There was no running water, and the family used an outhouse for a bathroom.

Everyone, including the family we were building for, worked hard throughout the first day. Around 4:00 p.m. we packed up our tools and told them we would be back to finish the house tomorrow.

The next day, we started with a prayer and got right to work. About mid-morning Andrea pulled me aside to meet the twin girls she had been playing with the past two days. Their family was living in a rusty, abandoned bus perched on a nearby hillside next to our build site. Andrea wanted to show me the bus people, so I walked over with her to take a look. Many of the windows were broken and all of the seats were gone. Inside was an old mattress propped up with cinder blocks to make it level because of the slope of the hill. I'm not sure how the bus got to that spot, because its engine was gone. Now the space under the hood was packed with wood and used as a cooking grill. It was remarkable what the family was able to do with so little. But it was a terrible place to live.

I returned to work, and at our lunch break I felt a tug on my shirt sleeve. Andrea looked up at me with a concerned expression and asked me a question that would change the course of our family's life. "Daddy, are you going to build a house for the bus people too?"

It was as if God himself were asking the question, and I could feel his Spirit touching my heart in a powerful way. I felt compassion for the bus family, but how could I say yes? Who would build the house? How would I work out all the details? I smiled at Andrea and gave her a hug and went back to working on the house we were building.

A few hours later, in a short but emotional dedication ceremony, our group handed the keys to a new home to the family we had been serving for the last two days. The final result of our hard work was right in front of us: a house that everyone could see and touch. Dave took a small piece of two-by-four board and got everyone to sign their names and write their favorite Scripture verse on it. Then we presented it to the family so they could remember our group. Many of us were crying as we said our good-byes.

As we drove off, they were already moving their few personal belongings into the new home. It was a heartwarming sight, and it gave us great satisfaction. This was everyone's first home build, and the weekend had a powerful relational quality. We developed a friendship with the family but also grew closer as a team. The building process connected us, and together we accomplished something greater than our individual parts ever could have.

Jesus certainly knew what to do with that $2,000 offering! I was so thankful to Sergio for his help in keeping the cost low and supervising the building process. We never would have been able to serve the family in such a way without his guidance.

As we traveled north over the border, I thought of all the occasions in the past when somebody had asked me, "What did you do this weekend?" So many times I responded, "Oh, not much" or "Nothing." In stark contrast, this weekend I had participated in something extraordinary. I liked the giving equation we had just used. Because of our efforts, a poor family would be warm and dry when it rained, and they would have a door to lock at night. Our group had helped transform a family's life, but in a way our lives were changed as well. Everyone in our group wanted to go back and build again.

When we rolled into YWAM Los Angeles late in the evening on Sunday night, I was tired from all the driving and working in the hot sun for two days. But I was full of joy as I shared with Janet about our fantastic weekend. As I crawled into bed, I knew I still needed to answer the question Andrea had asked me: "Daddy, are you going to build a house for the bus people too?"

I wanted to help, but where would I get the money? We had no tools and no plan in place. Who would build the house? I quickly fell asleep, resolved that if God wanted me to help build a home for the "bus people," he would show me how to do it.

SIX

Small Beginnings

"Expect great things from God, attempt great things for God."
William Carey

T H E next morning Janet and I enjoyed a cup of coffee together as I shared more details of the house build weekend. I told her how proud I was of Andrea and how well behaved she was on the trip. I also mentioned the family living in the old bus next door and how Andrea had asked me to build them a house too. We both knew there were youth groups coming to join us for the summer, and I wondered if maybe one of them would build the bus people a house.

Janet put down her cup of coffee and said, "You're good at communicating vision and always have creative ideas for how to get things done. With God's help, you'll figure it all out."

She was right. If God was involved in a project, it wasn't going to be a question of *if* the next house build would happen, but *when*.

The first phone call I made was to the leaders of a youth group from the Northwest that had come down to Mexico with us before. I shared my vision to build a home for the bus people. They thought it was an awesome idea, and they agreed to raise all the money to build the house.

I then asked Sergio if he would visit the bus family and verify that they did own the land and met all the criteria he normally used. As always, Sergio was eager to help. He confirmed the family's eligibility and also used his connections to get the concrete slab done and the building materials ordered.

A few months later the visiting team arrived in Tijuana and we built a house for the bus people. From what I could tell, the relational impact of this build experience was just as powerful as it had been for our YWAM team. The youth team grew closer through serving and discovered new joy in giving. The Mexican family receiving the new house was filled with joy too.

We began to recognize that God wanted us to keep building. Sergio called his work Casas de Amor, and I began wondering what we should call our new program. I knew the families felt loved by the building groups, but I could also see that the giving of the house produced a tremendous hope in the family about their own future. The more I thought about it, the more conviction came to me that we were hope builders as much as we were home builders. I thought "Homes of Hope" would be a perfect name for us to use. Not only did it convey a positive message, but it also captured the real spirit of what we were trying to do. I shared the idea with Janet, and she liked it too.

Over the next months, other youth groups heard about the opportunity to build for the poor and began signing up to join us. A new movement to serve the poor was slowly emerging. We knew that if we were going to keep growing the Homes of Hope program, we would need to put some supporting processes in place. Sergio was always happy to help, but I also knew he had his own ministries to oversee. We couldn't keep relying on him as we grew.

Our rental building in Playas de Tijuana was taking shape, as renovations had started on the kitchen, offices, and bathrooms. In the fall we were able to take down the wall of black felt and replace it with actual drywall. Our dorm rooms for women and men were outfitted with barracks-style bunk beds and could hold up to forty-five people in each room. We also built bathrooms with three sinks, three toilets, and three showers for the men and the same for the women. The sleeping arrangements were tight—triple-high bunk beds, each with a two-inch foam pad for a mattress. But this was luxury compared to what the El Florido families had.

Each level of growth required more resources and donations, and also more of my time and leadership focus. With the number of Homes of Hope builds increasing, it was becoming more difficult for Janet and me to supervise the Mexico outreaches from Los Angeles. Our family was also growing, as Janet was pregnant with our third daughter, Tiffany. We both liked living in Los Angeles, and neither of us was sure moving to Mexico was the right decision for our family. We were deeply rooted in the YWAM Los Angeles community, and none of our fellow staff members wanted to see us leave. At the same time, we were open to whatever God wanted us to do. We had a number of good young leaders who were working with us, and Janet and I debated whether one of them could move to Mexico to serve as the full-time outreach director while we continued to oversee everything from Los Angeles. We began sensing that we could be the ones who needed to move.

Our two young daughters, Rachel, seven, and Andrea, four, were open to it. Janet made it a priority to include them in our ministry travels, and they enjoyed our trips to Mexico. I don't remember ever having to ask more than once about going with us to Mexico, because my girls were always ready to go. In fact, anytime someone asked Andrea what she liked to do for fun, she responded, "I like to go to Mexico." Working with the poor was something special we did as a family.

In January 1991 I accepted an invitation to teach at several Discipleship Training Schools in India for two weeks. During one of my morning devotion times in India, I read Numbers 34, which speaks of the geographic inheritance God wanted to give to the people of Israel. The geographical description in Numbers 34 was eerily similar to that of San Diego County and Northern Baja, Mexico. I found myself asking, could God be using this scripture as a message for our family to move to Mexico? Did he have a new geographic inheritance for us?

After returning home from India, I couldn't wait to tell Janet about what I had read. She was typically more methodical than I was in making decisions, and she didn't jump to a conclusion. Although the Numbers 34 scripture was intriguing, the interpretation and meaning I was drawing from it was, of course, subjective. The question remained: Was another leader supposed to move down to Baja, or was this vision for us? God has often directed us through a series of guiding words, all woven together like a beautiful tapestry. This was one of those times.

As we continued to ponder the decision to relocate, John Dawson, now serving as a Southwest district leader for YWAM, announced a three-day strategy meeting to be held at the Lake View Terrace campus. The day before the meetings were to start, Janet had a dream she was talking about our future with a woman named Pat Eachus. Pat and her husband, Dick, led a six-hundred-acre YWAM campus in Richardson Springs, California. So the next day as the conference was starting, Janet asked Pat about getting together to talk, and Pat was delighted to do so.

Near the close of our time together, John Dawson led us in prayer for the Southwest district. As we all stood up to pray, my mind drifted to our work in Baja and our decision about moving to Mexico. I thought again about Numbers 34, and now a question formed in my mind: "Lord, is this vision for me or someone else?"

Suddenly from across the room, John Davidson, a fellow YWAM leader, interrupted the prayer meeting. "I have a word from the Lord for the Lamberts," he announced. Looking over at Janet and me, he declared, "This vision is for you and not for someone else." I was shocked. John used the very same words from my silent prayer only moments earlier! Only God could have arranged such a clear and distinct message for me to hear in such a remarkable manner. A surge of faith rose in my heart as I knew then we were to move. I turned to my left and made eye contact with Janet, and she was sitting down in her chair crying. She was seven months pregnant and was feeling overwhelmed at all the implications of a possible move.

Pat and Janet had not yet found the time to talk, and Pat sought out Janet and pulled up a chair next to her. "I know now what you wanted to talk to me about, and I have something from God for you," Pat said. "God knows that in your heart you are ready and willing to be obedient. You just need to know the details so you can fully obey. While we were praying, God gave me Numbers 34, which is all about your geographic inheritance. I think God wants to show you specifically where to live next."

It was another amazing confirmation from God. Pat had no idea that Janet and I had been meditating on Numbers 34 for guidance about our future. Pat was reading to Janet from the exact verses I had shared with her when I returned from India! John Davidson's message from God about this being a vision for us and Pat's encouragement to Janet from Numbers 34 gave us both a deep sense of peace about God's intent for our future. It was clear moving south was God's plan for the Lambert family.

In our follow-up discussions, Janet suggested that maybe we start out living in San Diego and not Baja, which was a new thought to me. The more we talked about the idea of pioneering a new YWAM expression in San Diego, the more right it felt. We would need an office that could handle group bookings, banking, and mail—things that would be key for our future growth. By establishing an office in San Diego, we would still have the ability to commute to Mexico in less than thirty minutes. An office in San Diego could also be key to helping us reach out to other nations. Janet and I both knew that our long-term calling was for many nations, not just one.

A few weeks later we drove to San Diego and decided the city's South Bay area was the ideal location to set up an office. We would call it YWAM San Diego/Baja, because both sides of the border were important, and they were linked together economically and geographically. The San Diego–Tijuana border is the largest international land border crossing in the world.

When I discussed the idea of opening a new YWAM San Diego/Baja location with Dave Gustaveson, he agreed to give us a good recommendation, but also he explained that we would need permission from the YWAM North America leadership team before moving forward with any new vision. "I imagine you've already thought this through in great detail," Dave said. "Have you drawn up a budget?"

The question caught me off guard. "I have not made a budget yet, but we'll have time to do that later."

Dave quickly added, "Don't wait too long; the budget will help you in your planning." I nodded my head in polite agreement. Dave continued, "You can run your finances through our LA nonprofit until you get your own nonprofit corporation set up. The LA base will send you out with a small offering, but that is as much as we can do right now. We have our own financial issues to deal with."

I hoped Dave couldn't see the shock in my face. Budgets, nonprofit corporations, administration—what was I getting into? All I wanted to do was mobilize youth and build homes for the poor. Adding to the stress of all the operational issues, Janet and I were uneasy about our own financial situation. Money had always been tight for us, but despite our low income in our ten years of marriage, we'd never had a bill we could not pay. To keep costs down, we had been living in half of a mobile home on the YWAM Los Angeles campus. A move south to San Diego with three children was probably going to be expensive. I also felt concern that the small car we owned wouldn't last much longer.

Our financial situation was in the front of our minds one evening as we drove west on the 118 freeway heading toward Northridge to visit friends from church. Rachel and Andrea were jammed in the back seat, making noise and kicking against the front seats.

"This car is too small for all of us," Janet said. "Why don't we pray and ask God to give us a bigger vehicle?"

"Okay, I will pray first, but I think you should pray too. God seems to hear you more than he does me."

"I think he hears us both just fine, but let's pray."

Praying always made sense to us. When we encountered difficulties, we'd take our concerns to God as a couple. Those simple prayers from our hearts always made a difference. We frequently experienced specific answers to those prayers. As we sped down the freeway, we asked God for a bigger vehicle.

About ten minutes later, we arrived at the home of our friends Jerry and Lenore Borelli. Jerry was a fun-loving East Coast transplant who had not yet lost his thick New Jersey accent. Lenore was an amazingly giving person, who would do anything for those who needed help. Not long after we arrived at their home, Jerry said, "Listen Sean, you see that nice Ford van parked on the other side of the street? If you want it, it's yours. We would like to give it to you because we don't need it anymore."

I looked out the window and spotted a large Ford van. I looked back at Jerry in amazement. "Jerry, just ten minutes ago Janet and I were praying for a larger vehicle. This is one of the quickest answers to prayer I have ever had." Jerry and Lenore were encouraged to be part of the story of God's provision for our family.

That summer I traveled to Chicago to seek approval from our North American leaders to start our new YWAM work. It was a formality for sure, but an important step in securing the use of the YWAM name. The North American leaders endorsed our vision, and they prayed over and commissioned me to start YWAM San Diego/Baja.

As soon as I found a phone, I called Janet to tell her the good news. Our next challenge would be finding a reasonably priced place for our family to live in San Diego. Ever the practical one, Janet began praying out loud in our kitchen from the moment I hung up the phone. "We have received great news, Lord, but where exactly will we live?" Just moments later the phone rang again, and Janet answered it.

"Hello, I am Chris Crane," the caller said. "You don't know me, but my wife Jane and I heard you want to start a YWAM base in San Diego, and we want to help. We will be out of town for about ten months, and we would like to offer our home for you and your family to live in to help you get started."

"That's very kind of you. And where in San Diego do you live, Chris?"

"La Jolla."

Janet swallowed hard. She knew that La Jolla was one of the nicest areas of San Diego.

"I am honored by your offer, but I'm sure our family can't afford to live in La Jolla."

"We intend to make it work for you," Chris assured her. "Please don't rent anything else before talking to me."

A few weeks later Janet and I drove down to San Diego to connect with Chris and Jane. We discovered they were not planning on getting a standard rental price for their home but only asked for whatever Janet and I could afford. I offered a feeble rent payment of $350 a month, which was slightly higher than what we were paying for our half a mobile home in Los Angeles. Chris graciously accepted my offer. Yet again the kindness of others was allowing us to continue forward on the path God had set for us. In October 1991 the Lamberts moved into the

Cranes' lovely four-bedroom home. We knew it wasn't long-term, but it would give us the landing pad we needed to get settled and allow us to look for some housing closer to the border.

The Los Angeles base gave us a $1,000 offering to help start YWAM San Diego/Baja. Since I didn't have any office equipment, I decided to first purchase a phone/fax/answering machine for $400, and with the remaining $600 I paid the next month's rent on the Playas property. Just like that, our new YWAM San Diego/Baja operation was out of cash—within forty-eight hours of starting! I was full of faith for our future, but it was also difficult to wrap my head around the looming financial pressures so early in our pioneering.

Sergio had helped us get the ball rolling by teaching us how to find families in need. I was a people builder, not a home builder, but I was committed to developing a repeatable building process for our visiting groups. I would often recruit professional builders to come and help us oversee the builds and get construction tips from them.

As we grew, we started to have multiple teams wanting to build a home for the poor at the same time. The growth was exciting, but we did not have enough tools for more than one group at a time to use. To save money, I started borrowing construction tools. At first this seemed liked a good idea, but over the course of the long workdays, many things got broken or lost. This put us in a difficult spot with the owners of the tools. We had to do the right thing and replace the lost or broken tools with brand-new ones. Ultimately this ended up costing us more than if I had gone out and bought them in the first place. It was a painful lesson. Pioneering has many challenges, and one of them is getting your processes stable and repeatable.

Short-term volunteers were the key to our operations. We did not have many staff, so I often recruited volunteer cooks, van drivers, builders, and translators to help with incoming groups. Transportation for the groups coming and going out to the work sites was perhaps our greatest challenge. We did not have enough money to buy our own vehicles, so we rented vans or a Mexican church's old bus. It was always a bonus when a visiting group said they would provide their own transportation.

We may have been underfunded and undertooled early on, but we were attracting increasing numbers of youth groups. We were now assisting a number of Tijuana-area churches and orphanages as well as needy families throughout the city. The fruit of our efforts to serve the Mexican people was obvious to all.

In retrospect, although we were growing, it was sloppy growth. Desperate to survive, I said yes to too many things and took on too much responsibility. My overall understanding of what it meant to be an effective servant leader was limited at best. I survived by working longer hours, but as time wore on, things started falling through the cracks and the ministry stress was mounting.

After staying in the Cranes' house in La Jolla for nearly a year, we moved our family to Chula Vista to be closer to the border. We operated the YWAM San Diego/Baja office out of the garage of our new rental house. We were economizing in every way we could imagine, but we were still having trouble making ends meet. The financial and administrative challenges we were facing were more complex than I had ever anticipated. I kept telling myself things would get better. I just had to find a way to make the budget work.

By December 1992 we were again out of money, and spring break, our next big income cycle, was still three months away. Night after night I toiled in our garage office until well after midnight, pounding away on the calculator, trying to figure out how to make ends meet.

One day I received an alarming call from John Liotti, our assistant director, informing me that the electric company in Mexico had turned off the power in our Playas outreach building. John and his wife, Melissa, had been with us from the beginning of our new ministry, and they were a gift from God. They had lived in the Playas building during its renovation even when the roof leaked and there was no heat. The Liottis often got sick because of the difficult living conditions, but they hung in there with us. John explained that to get the electricity turned back on, we would need to pay our outstanding balance of $1,500!

I didn't know where else to turn for help, so I scheduled a meeting with Chris Crane. Chris was empathetic about our predicament. Without hesitation he wrote a check to pay our delinquent electricity bill. I don't think I will ever be able to express how crucial Chris and Jane's support was in the founding years of our ministry.

The fact that we had managed to get the power turned back on did not solve the long-term financial crisis we were in. It just postponed it. I knew God had an answer for us, but I just didn't know what it was.

SEVEN

The Giving Formula

"It is more blessed to give than to receive."

Jesus Christ

IN January 1993 the skies opened up, drenching the Baja region with continuous rain. On January 11 the *Los Angeles Times* ran a story titled "Floods Leave Broken Lives in Tijuana." Tijuana's average annual rainfall is eleven inches, and we had fourteen inches in January alone! Walls of water filled with debris washed down the canyons and hillsides of Tijuana, wiping out many homes.

The hardest-hit areas were where the poor had built squatter shacks in dried-up riverbeds and vacant hillsides. The government of Tijuana was at a loss for how to help these displaced masses of people. They eventually moved most of them to an area called Via Verde on the eastern edge of the city. In this move they gave them an opportunity to own their own land. We had been working with city council members to ramp up our assistance to the people of Tijuana. Inspired by the huge need, I produced a short video about the dire situation. In it we invited groups to come soon to help alleviate the suffering in Tijuana. If ever we needed volunteers to build more Homes of Hope, it was now.

As a result, our numbers spiked that year. We built fifty homes for the poor, a record high. The volunteer groups typically ranged from eighteen to twenty-five people, and no previous building experience was required. We asked only that they come with a positive attitude and willingness to work.

With the new surge of groups building houses, we established more consistent work procedures. Each visiting team was assigned an "A" builder. An "A" builder was one of our staff who knew everything about how to build a house and was the on-site supervisor for the visiting group, guiding them through the entire build process. We also sent a "B" builder, who helped supervise various parts of the building process under the direction of the "A" builder. The visiting team's other needs were taken care of by one or two additional YWAM staff, who served as the team's host and translator, connecting the team to the family and the community we were building in. The work on-site was labor intensive—pounding nails, painting, lifting newly constructed walls, putting up drywall, and installing electrical wiring. We retained Sergio's guidelines of building only for families who had their own land rights, children, low income, and an obvious need for a new house. We also asked the families to help clear the site for the concrete slab and to work side by side with the visiting group.

Homes of Hope participants regularly reported to me that they received much more out of the building experience than they gave. Jesus Christ's words are as true today as they were two thousand years ago when they were first spoken: "It is more blessed to give than to receive" (Acts 20:35). Over the years our culture has reduced the meaning of this statement to primarily the giving of money. Allow me to restate the principle in a fresh and different way: *Only what you give to is what you get to keep.* This giving formula or principle works in all categories of life. If you don't give to your family and friends, you eventually will cease to have relationships with them. In education, the best teachers are those who help students receive the learning and also get it back out of them in creative ways. As students give away their learning, retention levels skyrocket. The giving formula is also true in our employment; if we don't give effort to our work, we will eventually lose our job. The giving formula is one of greatest principles I know for living a fulfilled life.

It is easy to look back and see the giving formula at work within the Homes of Hope movement. One of our former board members articulated it well when he said to me one day, "When you write a check, something is withdrawn from your account, but when you give of yourself, something is deposited in you." The benefits of giving to the poor are far bigger than we could have ever imagined when we started Homes of Hope. It has been amazing to see the reach and impact of Homes of Hope on both the poor and all those who have come to serve.

With each group that comes to build for the poor, there are often dozens more people back home who donated money to help pay for the home. With each house built, there are local neighbors who join in to help with the construction. Through Homes of Hope we have formed deep relationships with local pastors, community leaders, and government officials in the areas in which we build.

One of the main ingredients in our giving formula is that our response to the poor is rooted in relationships, not just resources. There is something powerful about standing shoulder to shoulder with a family in need and building a house *with* them, not just *for* them. Over a few days of working together, the poor become new friends. You now know them by name and have real relationships with them. At the dedication ceremony, when the keys are given for the new house, you truly feel like you're a part of their family.

In the early years, it took much longer to build a home because we included an upper loft over the two bedrooms and took time to mud and tape all the drywall seams. Mudding and taping requires some skill, and often our staff had to go back to finish it because the visiting group ran out of time to do it properly. Sending staff back to mud and tape took extra manpower and resources that we did not have.

One day I was in Home Depot and saw some one-inch-wide, eight-foot-long wood batten strips, and I thought to myself, "This would be perfect to cover over the drywall seams, and we could stop doing the mudding and taping." We tried it out and it worked great, so we started using them on every house. My wife now jokes with me that I can get a vision for something new even inside a Home Depot! Other small innovations came along the way, and over time we streamlined the whole building process. Veteran teams often find themselves finishing early, leaving more time to build relationships with the family or community.

I am often asked by those considering whether to do a Homes of Hope build if this is the *right* way to give. They wonder if it would be more efficient to just send money for the building materials and not bother showing up. As I look at God's response to our broken world, he didn't distance himself from our fallen humanity. He answered our brokenness relationally. He blessed us by sending his one and only Son, Jesus Christ, to reconcile us to the Father.

Relational answers in all areas of life are always the most powerful and long-lasting. Homes of Hope works because it's rooted in relationships, not just resources. As the visiting team serves alongside the family in need, their gift of relationship has a powerful impact on the family far beyond the resources given. The visiting team, the family, and our staff build together, eat together, cry together, and rejoice together. Our staff are trained to move relationally in the communities we are serving. Homes of Hope works because it is a partnership with the poor, not an impersonal, paternalistic handout that creates an ongoing cycle of dependency.

The question of how best to help the poor is complex and multi-faceted. Some people seem genuinely surprised when they learn there can be *wrong* ways to help those in need. Money in and of itself cannot solve the issue of poverty, because poverty is rooted in a wide variety of relational problems. We have broken relationships with God, with the planet, and with one another. One of the root causes of poverty in the developing world is corruption, which, if you think about it, is a relational problem. You can't have a prosperous society without a moral baseline. The issue of corruption related to poverty manifests itself in broken relationships. One human created in God's image oppresses and victimizes another human being who is also created in God's image.

If the giving formula being used does not possess the proper ingredients in the right amounts, it will not have its desired effect or impact. It's like making a cake—yes, you need all the correct ingredients, but you also need them in the proper amounts in order to produce a great-tasting cake. Money is one ingredient that can be used to help the poor, but money in and of itself will not break the cycle of poverty. The poor must be a partner in the process of the change they are seeking.

I learned from my good friend Kent Truehl, who teaches in many of our Community Development and Transformation schools within YWAM, what are commonly called the three stages of community development. They are *relief*, *rehabilitation*, and *development*.

Relief, which primarily involves one-way giving, is great if you're helping someone in a crisis, like victims of a war or natural disaster. In the short-term context of a crisis, one-way giving, or relief, is an appropriate response.

The next level, rehabilitation, has more complexity. Rehabilitation takes place when there is a mix of both local resources and some outside resources working together to achieve transformational change. This is exactly where Homes of Hope fits into the giving formula. We require that families in need take the first step to buy their own land before we will help them. They also have to clear the build site and work on the new house with the visiting team. It is a balanced and blended giving model, one in which the family is an equally vested partner in the transformational change process.

The third stage is development. True development is when the individuals or families in a community provide their own solutions, with little or no assistance from the outside. Within YWAM, I call this third stage our "Communities of Hope" vision. Our long-term goal is to see every community we partner with be engaged in its own long-term development. If too much one-way giving is reintroduced when a community is active in the third stage, it will ultimately retard the development of that community. Relief or one-way giving that goes on too long tends to create a paternalistic, top-down relationship with the poor. Then the poor begin to view themselves as only the receiver of help and not a vital part of their own transformational change. When there is too much one-way giving, recipients will soon come to expect and rely on the charity of others to survive, rather than working hard to improve their own future.

With every Homes of Hope family, I see fighters just like the ones Sergio described to me on our ride together through the *colonias*. These families have risked all of their savings to make a down payment on a small piece of land. They pay for that land every month for the next seven to ten years, using half or more of their meager income to make the land payments. These families are also willing to take another huge risk—tearing down their old house to make way for the new home. They work tirelessly for days to make sure their land is level before pouring the concrete floor. They wait for weeks for the volunteers to finally arrive and then work shoulder to shoulder with them to see the home built.

Historically, the giving formula embedded in Homes of Hope has had a powerful *hand-up* effect, rather than a *handout* effect. Families receiving a home are not sitting back and waiting for their free house to magically appear; they are joint-venture partners with us throughout the entire process.

There is always a lot to learn about poverty and how it affects individual families and their behavior. When you're poor, you throw your trash down into a canyon or burn it because you can't afford to both feed your family and pay for trash pickup. When you're poor, you think about how to get through the day or through the week, and the picture of your own future is dim and clouded, not bright and hopeful. In every Home of Hope dedication, families are given a new set of options and a fresh ability to think positively about their future. I love seeing the flame of hope rekindled. Hope is a powerful weapon to fight poverty with.

Over the years friends have given me books and news articles that have helped validate our Homes of Hope giving formula. One day Chris Crane forwarded me a *Wall Street Journal* article titled "Barrio Study Links Land Ownership to a Better Life."[1] Land titling was cited as a key ingredient in lifting people out of poverty. This was the very principle I had learned from Sergio years ago.

The Barrio Study, which was conducted by the Harvard Business School in association with two Argentine universities, focused on a Roman Catholic priest who led a large group of homeless families into San Francisco Solano, a one-square-mile area on the fringes of Argentina's capital, Buenos Aires. They constructed small homes using cardboard, metal, and scrap wood. These settlers hoped to gain land titles from the government, so they marked off thirty-by-one-hundred-foot lots and left room for future roads.

1. Matt Moffett, "Barrio Study Links Land Ownership to a Better Life," *Wall Street Journal*, November 9, 2005.

The Argentine government sent a bulldozer to destroy the homes, but a group of the squatters, mostly children and women, blocked the bulldozer's path, and the driver walked away. Eventually it surfaced that the land they were on was not government land but rather was held by thirteen private owners. As the story continued, half of the owners eventually accepted buyout offers, while the other half continued to argue over the financial terms.

Eventually, 419 families in San Francisco Solano had titles to their land, and 410 did not. According to the study, the families with land titles had nicer homes, their children stayed in school longer, and their daughters had a lower teen pregnancy rate. An interesting factor was that the income level of those who held land titles and those who didn't was approximately the same. However, those who knew they owned their land spent their money differently, parented differently, and viewed education differently. In a sense, they embraced long-term thinking about their own future, rather than the short-term thinking normally associated with abject poverty.

The results of the Barrio Study mirror many of the benefits we have observed in our Homes of Hope program. One of my favorite memories is a dedication ceremony with a forty-five-year-old man named Jorge with his wife and three children. As Jorge was given the keys to his new home, he sobbed with joy. "I am so happy today because now I have something to give my children when I die." The reality of his new home caused Jorge to think with optimism even beyond his death. With the keys to his new house in hand, he began envisioning what he would one day give his children as an inheritance.

Participation with dignity is vital, and we stress family participation throughout the build process. This includes the shopping trips in which our volunteers accompany them to local stores to select basic food supplies and clothing as a housewarming gift. We don't just buy it *for* them; we buy it *with* them.

During one memorable housewarming shopping trip with a family, Janet was walking through the grocery store with Martha, an energetic Mexican mother. Martha was told to pick out some food and other helpful items for her new home. As Janet and Martha made their way down the aisle pushing a shopping cart, Martha saw a metal grated washboard used for scrubbing clothes by hand. She turned to Janet with great emotion and asked if she could buy the washboard. Because Janet has her own washing machine at home, she wouldn't have thought about that as an important item to buy. Janet of course said yes, and Martha was delighted to have a new tool to wash her family's clothes with.

The family is the most important sphere of any society, and it is no surprise that where you find a breakdown of the family, you also find broken communities. The Homes of Hope program, with all its moving parts, has become much more than the building of four walls and a roof on top of a concrete slab. It is a builder of families. The gift of a home strengthens both families and communities.

EIGHT

Five Benefits of a Home

"God has given us two hands—one to receive with and the other to give with. We are not cisterns made for hoarding; we are channels made for sharing."

Billy Graham

WHAT I enjoy most about Homes of Hope is how it affects the recipient families' perception of God. The Bible says God is love, and you can see this as the family receives a home. They feel the love of God through the volunteers who come from far away to serve them in their time of need. Often participants have asked me if we make the families believe something in order to get a house. The answer is no, we simply love people. We freely give to the families based on their need, not what they say they believe. Homes of Hope is also unique because everyone who wants to serve the poor is welcome to build with us, no matter their spiritual background or beliefs.

It has been our custom from the first Home of Hope that we pray before every project for God's blessing and safety in building the house. We also pray at the end of the build during the dedication ceremony. The prayer times are optional for those who do not want to participate. We see these short prayer times as vital and a big part of our success. Over twenty-five years with thousands and thousands of volunteers, we have never had anyone get seriously hurt. Now that is an answer to prayer!

Over time we developed some core goals for every Homes of Hope family. We want every family

- to have the chance to hear the good news that God loves them and has a wonderful plan for their lives,
- to receive a Bible and the encouragement to know that in the Bible is wisdom and knowledge that is helpful for living one's life to the fullest,
- to be introduced to a church in their community where they can have ongoing fellowship with others, and
- to enjoy a new home that gives them sufficient shelter to raise their family in safety.

Homes of Hope is often the break a family needs to stop the drift into deeper poverty. I'm reminded of one couple in particular, Roberto and Maria. They had bought some land but could not afford both the apartment they had been living in and the land payments. So they decided to move onto the land. Roberto tried to build his own house, but the wind blew down the walls before he could secure them. A mechanic by trade, Roberto and his family started sleeping in an old taxi parked on their land, until he could figure out how to make his own house.

Roberto and Maria applied for a Home of Hope and were approved. The news of approval came just in time, as Maria was eight months pregnant. The family hoped to get into a new home before the birth, but the baby came early. Maria gave birth to little Emilia in the back of the old taxi all alone while her husband was off at work and her other children played outside. Shortly after the birth, a group from St. Louis built them a home. From time to time I visit the family, and it's remarkable to see what they have done with the house they were given. Homes of Hope transformed their lives.[1]

A question frequently asked by visiting groups is, "What happens to the family after we leave?" This is a great question, and several years ago we did our own study of prior Homes of Hope families. We

---

1. To view the video story of Roberto and Maria, go to www.ywamhomesofhope.org/taxi.

interviewed four hundred families, some who had lived up to ten years in their Home of Hope. We found that 93 percent of the people we built a home for were still living in the house. From our survey, along with information from countless follow-up visits by our staff and research from organizations like the World Health Organization (WHO), we developed a document titled "The Five Benefits of a Home." Following is our summary of the five benefits.

Economic Benefit

The gift of a basic home has a dramatic effect in helping leverage families out of their current economic situation. A solid, sufficient home provides both direct and indirect economic benefits. These include the opportunity to use the home for income-generating purposes. I have observed many of our Homes of Hope houses being used for small businesses, serving the needs of the community. In addition to living space, I've seen them used for hair salons, convenience stores, bakeries, wood shops, and the manufacturing of homemade craft products to sell. These home-based businesses become a crucial part of the family's income.

In addition, once a family is relieved of the burden of maintaining a self-built home with its constant need for repair, resources can be redirected to other needs such as health care, food, and education. Indirect economic benefits can also include fewer days missed from work or school, leading to better educational outcomes for children and increased dignity and self-esteem.

The overall economic impact of a family receiving a Home of Hope can be difficult to measure, because in every nation wages and material costs vary. I have done the math a few times, and it's safe to say that it would take an impoverished family seven to ten years to replicate what our volunteer groups do in just two or three days. The gift of a home has a profound economic impact on every family served.

Educational Benefit

A stable home environment encourages learning and promotes academic success. Children are more likely to attend and stay in school without the distraction and obstacles that accompany homelessness. There are many great websites with information on homelessness and its impact on children and their education. One of the best resources I found in my research is the National Alliance to End Homelessness (www.endhomelessness.org).

In Mexico it is common for the children of the poor to stop attending school around the age of twelve or thirteen (approximately seventh grade). With the family struggling to survive financially, the thirteen-year-old son or daughter is mature enough to find basic labor-intensive work, like washing cars, recycling, or helping parents with their trade. The short-term savings in school expenses, combined with the extra income the young adolescent is now earning, feels significant to the family. However, the truth is that these children will find themselves trapped at the same level of employment as they get older. Foreign factories (*maquiladoras*) typically like to hire workers with a minimum of a ninth-grade education. Workers who have dropped out of school before this point are at a disadvantage in their future employment options. Children who come back to a home that the family owns are more likely not only to attend school more often but to excel in their studies and stay in school longer.

One such example is Tania, who at age thirteen was living with her mom, dad, and two siblings at her grandma's house. Her family owned land nearby but was staying with Grandma to save money to pay for the land. They hoped to build a new home on it. One day Tania's family came home to find all their possessions in the street. Grandma, who was very poor herself, could no longer accommodate them. With nowhere else to go, the family was forced to live on their vacant land with no shelter from the elements.

Over the next few weeks the family's situation grew worse. Tania's dad was bitten by a dog one night and could no longer work. Because of the loss of his income, the family often went hungry. Tania's mom lost a baby she was carrying due to all the stress. Tania decided to drop out of school and start working to help her family. Her mom, however, told her to stay in school, and shortly after reaching their lowest point, the family was approved for a Home of Hope. I learned later that six months after receiving their new home, Tania graduated first in her class at school. I find it hard to tell her story without crying. Because of the crisis in her family, this bright young girl had almost dropped out of school. Receiving a Home of Hope helped stabilize Tania's family and gave her a chance to succeed. Stories like Tania's are what I live for. I love engaging a broken world with God's generosity.[2]

Health Benefit

I often tell visiting groups that if all we did was put in solid floors for people to live on, we would still transform many lives. One study conducted by the World Bank and the University of California at Berkeley evaluated a Mexican government program that replaced dirt floors in homes with concrete. The results were astounding. There was an immediate 78 percent reduction in parasitic infections and 49 percent reduction in episodes of diarrhea. The children also showed up to a 96 percent improvement in cognitive development.

When poor families build shelters from discarded wood and other items, they sometimes unknowingly expose themselves to toxic chemicals that threaten their health. Poor lighting or extreme temperatures in these structures also affect the human body in negative ways.

Indoor air pollution in makeshift shelters contributes to respiratory and cardiovascular diseases. The World Health Organization, in a report titled "Household Air Pollution and Health," estimates that nearly 4.3 million people a year die prematurely from illness attributed to household pollution from unventilated wood or coal stoves.[3] In other words, the poor are literally dying in an attempt to stay warm or cook a meal. These pollutants, along with dampness and mold, often factor into the development of allergies and asthma. Families in many housing situations are also living nearly on top of one another, and the overcrowding leads to the spread of bacteria and viruses.

Another clear benefit of better health is a reduction in days missed from work and school. One of the great joys in my life is to go out and visit a family that has received a Home of Hope about six to eight

2. To view the video story of Tania and her family, go to www.ywamhomesofhope.org/tania.
3. World Health Organization, "Household Air Pollution and Health," updated February 2016, http://www.who.int/mediacentre/factsheets/fs292/en/.

weeks after their house has been completed. On one of my follow-up trips, I talked with a family of five that had been living in a scrap-wood structure with a dirt floor and a blue tarp for a roof. I was holding the couple's nine-month-old baby when the mother said, "My husband no longer misses work, because he's not sick anymore." Then with a big smile she declared, "And my baby is not sick anymore either."

This was yet another example that when the family is healthy and well rested, each member can excel in his or her job or schooling. In remaining healthy, the family saves significantly on medical expenses, they are more productive, and they contribute more to their surrounding community.

Transformed Thinking Benefit

The small structures we build may not impress some people, but to families in poverty they are a dream come true. To go from a dirt floor to concrete, and from a leaky tarp to a real roof, is truly life changing. Not only do these upgrades create obvious physical benefits, they also spark transformational thinking. The poor begin viewing themselves and their future differently. At its core, poverty is an inability to accurately perceive one's own future.

Impoverished families without a home often question their worth and have difficulty breaking out of a day-to-day survival mentality. When a family achieves basic sufficiency in their housing, they begin to dream about their future. A home not only provides identity in the community; it also provides a safe and welcoming environment for families to raise their children.

The Lambert family saw this impact firsthand when my six sisters and brother, along with their spouses and kids and my family, decided to participate in a home build to celebrate my parents' fiftieth wedding anniversary. We originally intended to throw them a big party, but my mom said, "No, I don't want a big party. I would rather have everyone go to Mexico and build a home for the poor to celebrate."

On Christmas Eve 2007, twenty-seven of the Lambert clan gathered around a precious Mexican family and gave them the keys to their new house. The family had been living on dirt for more than ten years.

At the close of the dedication time, the thirteen-year-old daughter of the family walked up and handed my mother a handwritten note that read in part, "Thank you so much for giving my family a house. I'm so excited today because now I can invite my friends over to play." Up until that point in her young life, she had been so embarrassed by the way her family was living that she had never had a single friend over to play with her. It was an impactful family memory, one that I will always remember.

As reported in the Barrio Study, a home built on land the family owns produces healthy, long-term thinking, helping to break the cycle of poverty.

Spiritual Benefit

The gift of a home is a practical demonstration of God's love for a family in need. The God I know is a personal God who loves his creation deeply. Unconditional love, however, is often difficult for a person in poverty to comprehend.

Josue Ochoa, one of our longest-serving staff members, tells a wonderful story about a family of five that he helped with a new Home of Hope. The wife was several months pregnant with her fourth child, and their living situation was desperate. She had applied for a Home of Hope, but her husband was skeptical and passive. He told Josue, "I don't understand why someone would give us a house. The only person who has ever given me anything is my own mother."

When the application was completed, Josue did a site visit to verify they needed help with a new home. After the visit, Josue was confident the family qualified for help, and with great joy he informed the husband and wife that they would be getting a new home. The mother was deeply thankful, but the father was still skeptical. His emotions quickly turned to anger, and he pointed his finger at Josue. "Did you get my wife pregnant? Is that your baby? Is this why you're being so nice to my family?"

Josue calmly answered that he was not the father of their child and explained we were there to help him because we were filled with the love of God, and we wanted him to know that same love.

A few weeks later, the house was being built by a bunch of joyful teenagers from Oregon. After the dedication ceremony, everyone could see the father was overcome with emotion, and one of the group leaders pulled the man aside to talk to him.

Through a translator he said, "Today you have the opportunity to get two houses. The first is a wood house that your family can live in for many years. The second is an eternal house that Jesus is building for you in heaven." He shared with the husband from the Gospel of John, when Jesus tells his worried disciples, "Do not let your hearts be troubled. You believe in God; believe also in me. My Father's house has many rooms; if that were not so, would I have told you that I am going there to prepare a place for you? And if I go and prepare a place for you, I will come back and take you to be with me that you also may be where I am" (John 14:1–3).

Jesus is the ultimate home builder. He builds us eternal homes because he is moving relationally to reunite us with the Father in family love. In my view, Homes of Hope is one of the best ways to communicate the love of God to families in need.

NINE

Pruning

"Never mistake activity for achievement."

John Wooden

IN our first few years of pioneering YWAM San Diego/Baja, we were enjoying steady growth. However, this progress came at a price and exposed the lack of depth in my operational leadership skills. It was one thing to run a program but something entirely different to oversee a whole organization. Growth meant adding more staff, teams, meals, transportation, housing, tools, and vendors, plus more bookkeeping and board governance. I lacked the proper leadership skills to handle the increased workload.

As one youth build team was leaving, another was typically on the way, giving everyone only a few hours of transition time to prepare for their arrival. Our pricing model was insanely heroic; we boasted that we delivered the most services for the least amount of money. The accounting system in place was wobbly at best, and it was often hard to tell if we were operating in the red or black. To keep costs low we relied heavily on our staff, who assumed the responsibility of multiple jobs. At the same time we all found it hard to get time off to rest. I was pushing to book every extra team I could squeeze into the schedule, to help generate more income to pay our bills. I encouraged staff to press on, thinking if we could just get through the next spring break or summer program, we would be okay. But extra growth brought extra expenses and further exposed our flawed pricing model.

To help stabilize our situation I reached out to my friend Joe Matta, a good businessman who, with his wife Kay, had joined the staff of YWAM Los Angeles. Joe began helping us with bookkeeping and accounting. Joe's efforts were starting to make a difference, but he was commuting from Los Angeles one or two days a month, which was not enough to sort out all of the financial chaos I had created. I was convinced that our holy grail was *low prices and great service*. I didn't want anyone to think we were building homes for the poor to make money. I didn't know what things were costing us because we were operating with poorly designed account codes that generated incomplete financial reports.

In an attempt to keep costs low for the groups and save money, we acquired our own forestry permit from the Mexican government and started trucking our own wood across the border into Mexico rather than using a Mexican lumber yard. While this saved a few dollars in the short term, the process took up our staff's time, which meant we were all dropping the ball in other areas of our responsibilities. Our cash flow was erratic. We would surge with income in spring and summer when most of our youth teams would show up. Then in the fall and winter we would try to hang on until the next spring and summer cycle.

During one stretch when the bills were piling up, we found ourselves way over our heads with debt. Around that time, I received a personal credit card solicitation in the mail with four blank checks. It was still a number of months until our next big income cycle, and I told myself if we could just hang on for a little while longer, we could make it. So I decided to use one of the credit card checks to make a loan to YWAM, telling our leaders that YWAM could pay me back when more teams arrived and we had more cash flow.

A few months later when the team monies came in, I paid off the credit card debt but found that we were short on funds in other areas. I repeated the credit card loan process several more times, each time able to pay back the loan. It was high risk, and I knew it. Fortunately, YWAM in Chico, California, made us a more formal bridge loan to help us make it through the next cycle or two, but soon we would need to pay that loan back too.

Our problems carried over into the summer of 1994, and our growth remained erratic and unorganized. Janet was becoming more concerned about the repeated borrowing and excessive workloads. We clearly were underfunded and understaffed.

We kept going because our programs had lots of life in them. First-time teams were becoming yearly alumni, and we had lots of raving fans. The youth group leaders would often tell me that the most impactful thing they would do each year was to partner with YWAM in our youth outreach program and build a home for the poor.

By August everything started to unravel. One of my key leaders confessed to me he had a drug addiction problem, and we had to dismiss him. Week after week, staff members announced they were leaving, including John and Melissa, the directors of our Playas campus. The crazy work hours, chaotic growth, and stressful financial environment had taken their toll on all of us. The staff who were leaving all had well-thought-out reasons to go. I knew deep inside that we were a sinking ship, and they were jumping off before we went under. At the end of the summer, our operations were a huge mess. We were swimming in unpaid bills, and our debt had ballooned to nearly $50,000. Worse yet, it would be seven months until our next big income cycle at spring break!

Only three years earlier I had moved with my young family to the border region, determined to build a great ministry that honored God and served people. Now it was all imploding. I was getting phone calls from other YWAM leaders who were concerned about our situation. Apparently many of the departing staff had written letters and made calls complaining about my leadership. My confidence was at an all-time low. Packing up and quitting was starting to look like my best option. I thought, *Everyone else is leaving, so why shouldn't I?* Depression was nagging at my soul, and it felt like someone had twisted my insides and turned them upside down. I am naturally a happy and optimistic person, but at that time I was on the edge of an emotional breakdown.

Our YWAM office now was in a dark and moldy landing area by the stairs of a house we were renting. Janet had her computer and office tucked into the tiny laundry room just a few feet away. As I sat at my office chair watching Janet working at her computer, I felt totally overwhelmed and began to weep.

"I failed us. I led us to this place, and nothing is working. It's time to do something different. What would *you* like to do?"

Janet's green eyes now brimmed with tears. I wanted whatever we did next to be her decision since I felt like such a failure as a leader. When she didn't speak right away, I glibly suggested we move to Yakima, Washington, since she had family there. I thought she would like that idea, but all it did was signal to her that I was done, ready to quit. Janet could see the defeat in my face and started to cry too. Then she made a statement that would radically change the rest of our lives.

"I just want to be in the will of God. If we quit now, I believe Homes of Hope will end too, and a lot of families will miss out on the future blessing of a home."

Her words had a deep conviction, and as she spoke them, they strengthened me. "I just want to be in God's will too," I blurted out through my tears.

Our present situation was grim, but Janet's willingness to keep going gave a much-needed spark of optimism about our future. As we prayed together, we recalled the Numbers 34 scriptures and the word God had given us: "This vision is for you and not for someone else." God had given us the San Diego/Baja area as our inheritance in YWAM. If we gave up now, there would be nobody to take our place.

It was clear we needed to reboot our efforts and get some management help. I considered myself a likeable leader of good character, but my leadership skill level was modest at best. I knew that if I didn't get some help, we certainly would crash and burn.

So I called a friend from Oregon, Pastor John Bauer. I started our conversation grousing about all the financial problems and blaming everything that had happened on others. Pastor John and his church had partnered with us many times. He was a faith-filled leader who had always been an immense source of encouragement to me. That's why I had reached out to him. He listened to me for a few minutes and then interrupted, "The way I see it, Sean, is everything that has happened is your responsibility, and you are simply not owning it. You're not seeing your own leadership flaws." I listened in silence as Pastor John continued to speak to me in a sharp and direct manner. "You need to quit complaining about what everyone else has been doing and take a fresh look at your own leadership. I think the problem is with you, not everyone else."

I was stunned by Pastor John's tone and sat silent for a few moments, not sure how to respond.

"Look, Sean, trust me in this. Once you fully own your situation and stop making excuses, you'll be able to achieve twenty-twenty vision in your leadership. God will show you what to do next and how to rebuild your ministry, but you have to accept responsibility for what has happened. Think about what I am saying, and we can talk again in a few days."

As I hung up the phone, I was angry at my friend's blunt assessment of my leadership. I was hurting, struggling, and I had anger and resentment toward many of the staff members who had quit on me. How could John's assessment be right? Was I blaming everyone else for problems I created? Had I become blind to my own leadership weaknesses?

As my frustration level died down, I had a growing sense that John had said exactly what I needed to hear. Sitting at our small kitchen table, I finally prayed the prayer that would open my eyes and change the course of my leadership journey. "God, if what Pastor John is saying to me is true, you show me."

I had barely finished the short prayer when a strong impression popped into my mind. I sensed the Lord was saying I should read the staff file of the leader we had asked to leave because of his addiction problem. This leader was talented, but he also caused a lot of damage to our ministry in his departure. I quickly pulled out his file, and my eyes fell on a reference letter from his pastor that I had read when we accepted him on staff. I was both stunned and convicted as I read it. The pastor's words were gracious and complimentary about the man's skills and ability to contribute, but the letter was also full of warnings and cautions. In part, his comments read, "Do not give him too much leadership too quickly, and do not overwork him. He has a history of drug addiction, and under stress he will revert to those addictions."

The information in the letter, combined with Pastor John's exhortation to accept responsibility for what had happened, made me realize I had to change. I had done everything the reference letter had warned against doing. I had put the work of the ministry above the health of the staff member. I had not led him properly, and he was unable to grow within the ministry. Under the stress of our crazy workload, he turned back to his addictions.

The next few days were filled with more revelations as I continued to examine and accept responsibility for my own leadership actions. Looking back, the busier we had become as a ministry, the more I cut corners to get things done. I had not given enough of my time to mentoring and developing the staff. At first it was hard looking inward and owning my mistakes, but the more I owned what had happened, the more hope it produced in me. I went from a blurry-eyed leader who was filled with excuses to a hope-filled leader with fresh twenty-twenty vision. I was hopeful I could make all the changes necessary to rebuild the ministry.

God was also giving revelation to Janet about how we were to rebuild the ministry. To help with our support, she was working part-time from home as a medical transcriptionist. Janet would typically get up at 4:00 a.m. and work for a few hours before the rest of the family started their day. One afternoon, while on her way to drop off some of the work at a medical center, she found the entrance blocked by a twenty-foot tree that had split down the center. Once Janet was inside, the manager of the medical center approached her. "Did you see the tree?" she asked.

"Yes," Janet said. "I've never seen one split into three pieces like that."

"If those trees don't get pruned properly, they just fall apart."

Janet stood in silence and thought about the manager's statement. It was a divine moment of revelation as she felt the Lord speak to her in a quiet way: *"And that is just what I am doing with you, Sean, and this ministry. You are being pruned so you can bear more fruit."* When Janet returned home, she read what Jesus said in John 15:2: "He cuts off every branch in me that bears no fruit, while every branch that does bear fruit he prunes so that it will be even more fruitful."

The next morning over coffee, Janet shared her revelation concerning the tree and God's pruning with our dear colleagues Andy and

Marcia Zimmermann, who were visiting us from Ventura. Andy, who grew up in Switzerland, said he had learned about the importance of proper pruning and gardening from his grandfather and father. "Whenever I prune a tree, someone usually freaks out and tells me I killed it," he said. "They always think I have gone too far. But I smile because I know pruning is the best way to produce sustained fruit. If you want good fruit, you have to prune a tree. If you just want green growth, you don't need to prune the tree."

This revelation showed Janet and me that our ministry was still alive because God, in his faithfulness, had decided to prune us before it was too late! I resolved that we were going to prune and re-pioneer the ministry in a healthy way.

I gathered the remaining staff in our Playas building to talk about setting a new course for the future. I opened the meeting by acknowledging my leadership failures and releasing everyone from any sense of prior commitments they had made to the ministry. I told them they were free to move on if they wanted. I told them what Janet and I had learned about pruning and about God's heart that we keep going and bear good fruit. I said we were no longer going to fall into the routine of doing too many things all at once. In moving forward we would focus on our two core callings: youth teams and Homes of Hope.

Over the next week I had one-on-one conversations with the remaining staff, working through potential next steps. When all was said and done, five staff members decided to stay on with us. We were starting over, and this time we would build slower and with more intentionality.

Perseverance is an underrated leadership quality. When times are tough, it is so easy to get discouraged and want to quit. Galatians 6:9 says, "Let us not become weary in doing good, for at the proper time we will reap a harvest if we do not give up." I was fortunate to have Janet as my partner, for in my time of weakness she was strong. Since the day we got married, she has been a constant source of encouragement to me, never wavering from our calling to serve the Lord. Janet would often say, "We are pioneering, so we can't quit! If we don't give up, we are going to see God do everything he wants and a lot more than we expect!"

A few weeks after our crisis, I phoned Chris Crane to report on the ministry and thank him for helping us. I also had some questions about finances and pricing that I wanted to discuss with him. Chris is a graduate of Harvard Business School and an invaluable source of inspiration and knowledge. After I gave an update on all we had been through, I asked him questions about pricing. "Chris, we have plenty of teams coming in, but the math is simply not working out. Since we are a Christian ministry, I am sensitive about our pricing. I don't want anyone to think we are doing this for money."

Chris paused for a moment and then asked, "Does anyone complain about your pricing?"

"No," I answered proudly. "In terms of short-term missions, nobody offers what we do and charges so little."

"And that is your problem."

"What do you mean?"

"Normally, if you don't have at least 20 percent of the people saying you're too expensive, then you are *not expensive enough*. If you do not change your pricing model now, Homes of Hope will cease to exist in the future."

"But if we raise our prices, I am afraid people will stop coming."

"Listen," Chris said calmly, "if you don't raise your prices, you won't be around much longer and then *everyone* will be disappointed anyway. Your groups will understand the need for these increases." Chris sensed that I still lacked the inner confidence in my leadership to raise our prices, so he kept challenging me. "If you had more money, what would you do with it?"

I thought for a moment and responded with a list of things we could do to improve our program, such as upgrading our vans, offering better-quality food, and improving team housing. Before I could finish my list, Chris stopped me.

"So if you raise your prices, you'll be able to offer even better and more consistent services than you are right now. And you will be able to pay all of your bills on time and still have funds left over to even out your cash flow in slow periods and also have funds set aside for emergencies."

The thought of never borrowing money again sounded wonderful. I knew in my heart what Chris was telling me was right. I had the flawed idea that because of the nature of our charity work, we should only charge exactly enough to pay for basic operating costs. While that sounded noble, it was naive thinking. With our poor budgeting model, our pricing didn't take into consideration costs such as phones, computers, professional services, or even simple things like gas to go visit a family that received a house. The only reason we'd survived was that our staff served way above the call of duty. It was clear to me now that by not placing enough value on our staff's time and effort, we had caused them to become discouraged and leave.

The discussion with Chris strengthened my resolve to raise our prices. I reached out to Joe Matta again, and we started over by rebuilding our account codes and creating a well-thought-out formal budget. After going through a proper budgeting process, it became obvious that our pricing was almost *half* of what it should have been! No wonder we had spent three years living in debt and cutting corners trying to make ends meet. I was still nervous about the effect our price increase would have on our overall group numbers, but I had to do it. I couldn't keep sitting up late at night in a futile effort to make all the financial numbers work. So I dramatically raised our prices. And just as Chris had predicted, there was an immediate improvement at nearly every level of our programs.

Janet and I, along with our team of five, aggressively attacked the remaining debt. We decided to take back anything we had recently bought that was still returnable. One of our staff had purchased an expensive gas grill at Home Depot to cook hot dogs for our youth teams. The grill had only been used two times, so we cleaned it up and pleaded with the manager of Home Depot to take it back. And he did! We sold a van and returned some new tools that we were not using. We put all these funds toward our debt. We also took an offering among ourselves. I figured if we were not willing to give to the ministry, how could we expect others to? We had some surprise donations come in, and new teams signed up to join us in the fall and winter quarters. With everyone's focus and commitment, we were debt-free within six months! And despite the price increase, our team numbers grew 20 percent over the prior year.

Crises in our lives can bring great clarity, and humility allows us to receive wisdom from others, causing ever faster growth. I learned that leaders don't have to do everything; they just need to make sure everything gets done. Great leaders develop teams around them that have both complementary abilities and a willingness to sacrifice individual glory in order to achieve authentic success as a team. I was strong in vision and programs but weak in finances and administration. I had to learn how to build an effective team, one that shared our vision and could help carry the load.

Pastor John's exhortation to look at my flaws led me to reach out regularly to other leaders for advice and wisdom. While driving back and forth to Mexico, I listened to teaching tapes from leadership experts such as John Maxwell. I became an avid reader, devouring leadership books to help me grow. My new passion for learning brought with it even more anticipation for our future growth as a ministry. We had gotten this far by applying faith and obedience to what we knew to be God's call on our lives. This next season would be no different.

TEN

Fruit That Remains

"Faith is to believe what you do not see; the reward of this faith is to see what you believe."

Saint Augustine

YWAM San Diego/Baja was now exhibiting all the signs of healthy growth we had hoped for—new staff, more teams, more income, and increasing numbers of completed homes. For the second year in a row, we completed more than fifty Homes of Hope, the majority of which were located in Via Verde, the area filled with hundreds of families affected by the 1993 flooding. One of our key partners in Via Verde was Pastor Alvin, who had a growing church that practiced the same two-handed approach of sharing God's love that YWAM used. In addition to rendering much-needed spiritual aid through their church services, they regularly hosted medical clinics and distributed food and clothing.

Pastor Alvin lived in Via Verde, so he was also helpful in identifying qualified families for our Homes of Hope program. YWAM's assistance to the flood victims and partnership with city council members in serving the poor led to us getting public recognition from the mayor's office in Tijuana. These community-based partnerships, fueled by energy and resources from the visiting volunteer teams, were having a transformational impact on Via Verde.

Meanwhile, north of the border, our family's housing situation grew more tenuous. The owner of our rental house in Chula Vista, California, decided to move back into his property, so we were forced to look for a new place to live. We eventually found a new rental house a few miles away. It was a nicer home and more expensive, but we were happy to get out of the moldy basement of our prior rental. We accepted the move as part of the price we knew we had to make to pioneer this work. But unbeknownst to us, God had something much better in store for our family.

A few days after Christmas, I was sorting through the YWAM mail when I noticed a letter with no return address. I was stunned by what I found inside. There was a $25,000 check made out to YWAM, designated for our personal support, with specific instructions that the money be used for us to buy a home! The note stated, "The Lambert family has been instrumental in seeing other families receive a home. We want their family to have a home of their own." I inspected the check over and over again because I couldn't believe it was real. There was no donor listed, so I assumed they wanted to remain anonymous. Whoever it was had seen us help poor Mexican families get a new home, and God had put it on their heart to help us get one of our own.

I couldn't wait to show Janet the check. I plotted the whole way home how to prank her, but when I walked into the house, the news was simply too joyful to ruin with some kind of joke. I found Janet in the kitchen.

"Something arrived in the mail for us," I said, unable to hide my goofy grin. I handed her the letter and check then stepped back to watch her reaction.

"What?" she asked, reading the letter. "This is amazing!" Janet's face lit up like a fireworks display, and she kept repeating, "Thank you God! Thank you God!"

We started looking right away to find a house to buy, but it was harder than we thought it would be. Because of our low income, the bank wanted a larger down payment. Over the next few months, I reached out to some of our core supporters, and they helped us increase the size of our down payment to satisfy the bank. Finally, in August 1995, after fifteen years of marriage, which began with us living in one room together, our family was able to have a home of our own! We bought a modest 1,350-square-foot, two-bedroom, one-bathroom home with a detached garage and another small building in the backyard. The previous family had used it as a playroom for their kids, but we knew it could be made into an ideal guesthouse. Janet and I took one of the bedrooms, and our three daughters lived in the other. When our youngest daughter, Tiffany, asked Janet how long we were going to be staying in this new house, Janet replied, "At least until you graduate from high school." Tiffany, age four, thought Janet was teasing her because we had already lived in six different places since she was born.

During this time, the words of Jesus in Luke 12:31 gained a new meaning for us: "But seek his kingdom, and these things will be given to you as well." Janet and I had trusted God in joining YWAM, getting married, having children, and eventually starting YWAM San Diego/ Baja. We had committed our lives to serving others and building homes for the poor, and now God, through an anonymous donor, had blessed our family with a home as well. Our motive was never giving to get but to be a blessing to others. We were rich in family, rich in friendships, and rich in our relationships with the poor. It was a joy to give to others, and our lives were more fulfilled than we could ever have imagined.

Many might be surprised that the Bible teaches that there are two judgments after we die. One is a judgment of association: Did we have a relationship with the Lord through a confession of faith (Romans 10:9–13)? The second is a judgment of works: What did we do with the life God gave us (1 Corinthians 3:10–13)? The Bible is clear that God will reward all of us for the life we live, and these rewards can come here on earth or in eternity. I own several biographical books about missionaries who lived lives of sacrifice and service to God. Although they did not receive much in the way of earthly rewards, they are now receiving great reward for all eternity. Janet and I had always banked on most of our rewards being collected in heaven, but we were truly thankful for the gift of our own home here on earth.

Homes of Hope was also starting to get some recognition from other leaders in the YWAM world. One of those leaders was Jose Curial from YWAM Guadalajara. Jose and his wonderful wife, Adriana, were working to make a difference in Mexico's second-largest city. We were now getting requests from alumni groups about building Homes of Hope in other parts of the world. It seemed like a logical step to partner with Jose and expand Homes of Hope into Guadalajara.

To lay some groundwork before any volunteer teams arrived to the city, Jose and I decided to host a community-wide pastors' breakfast. More than fifty leaders attended. During the breakfast we cast the vision of bringing in hundreds of youth to serve the greater Guadalajara area and asked each pastor to fill out a response form indicating their needs, as well as their interest level in partnering with us. Overall, the response was fantastic. We had more offers for partnership than we could act on.

During one of my site visits to Guadalajara, Jose took me to visit a poor community called Santa Maria. The living conditions there were as bad as anything I had observed in Baja. It was hard to imagine people living in such deplorable conditions. When we began bringing teams to Guadalajara, one of our main focuses was to build Homes of Hope in Santa Maria. Wood was expensive in Guadalajara, so we decided to build with metal studs, combined with normal drywall on the inside, and all-weather fiber cement for the exterior siding. The plan worked well, and over the next few years we built 128 homes for the poor in Guadalajara. At the same time, we sent outreach teams to many other parts of the city.

Shortly after starting Homes of Hope in Guadalajara, Steve Tackett, the leader of YWAM Nashville, expressed an interest in building Homes of Hope in Cancún, Mexico. Cancún is known as a beautiful resort and tourist destination, but not far from the lush accommodations of the resorts is tremendous poverty. Steve later told me that for every hotel room in Cancún, they need to hire four low-wage workers to do housekeeping, food service, and maintenance. These workers live on the edges of the city in rundown houses or makeshift shelters that tourists rarely, if ever, get a chance to see.

Pushing into these new regions was timely because our Tijuana programs were very full, and some weeks we were turning groups away. In addition to the spring and summer youth teams, we started having large numbers of weekend teams wanting to build in the fall and winter quarters. We were now hosting more than three thousand people annually. To think that Janet and I had worked for the entire year of 1987 and managed to get only eighty participants to join us!

Since starting back in the 1980s, we had used basic names when referring to our youth group trips, such as "Spring Break Outreach" or "Summer Short-Term." We knew it was time to put a more dynamic designation to these youth outreaches that had grown so much over the last ten years. Just like with Homes of Hope, other YWAM leaders were interested in replicating what we were doing with our youth mission trips. We decided we needed a common name that unified the vision and decided on the name Mission Adventures.

The Mission Adventures program we created has two core focuses. The first is to invest in training and discipling the youth. In each Mission Adventures event, we provide a guest speaker, high-energy worship, and an overall theme. The second focus of the program is to engage the youth in various hands-on outreach efforts, teaching them to love their neighbor. We often use creative arts such as dramas, dance, music, puppets, or children's programs to communicate the good news of God's love to others. We also do acts of service, such as building Homes of Hope, working in an orphanage, or helping with a community service project. The Mission Adventures staff takes care of all the program and administrative responsibilities, allowing the youth leaders to focus on the outreach and on building relationships with their youth.

A core principle that makes Mission Adventures work can be found in James 1:22: "Do not merely listen to the word, and so deceive yourselves. Do what it says." I often joke that Nike owes the Bible some serious royalty money for the "Just do it" slogan! The message of "Just do it" is not only true in athletics; it is also true in our spiritual growth.

In January 1997 we hosted a three-day international conference at our Tijuana center to roll out our new name and youth training concepts. About thirty YWAM leaders from around North America accepted our invitation to attend. We started the conference by first listening to what these leaders were already doing in various areas of youth training and outreach. Then we presented the Mission Adventures concept and invited others to join us in what amounted to a free franchise. We gave away all that we had learned to anyone that was interested in joining the Mission Adventures movement. We also presented the group with a how-to document outlining all the core elements of the program. This would serve as a guide for other YWAM centers wanting to start their own Mission Adventures program.

With the launch of the Mission Adventures Network, youth participation over the next few years went from three thousand a year to over nine thousand. Our combined Mission Adventures and Homes of Hope networks were now multiplying our ministry to youth and the poor around the world.[1]

1. To find out more about our Mission Adventures youth program, go to www.mission adventures.net.

ELEVEN

Matters of Life and Death

"Speak up for those who cannot speak for themselves, for the rights of all who are destitute."

Proverbs 31:8

I N February 1997, Chris Crane contacted Janet and me about hosting a Homes of Hope tour in Tijuana for attendees of a Vision and Values Conference presented by the Young Presidents Organization (YPO) at the Torrey Pines Sheraton in La Jolla, California. YPO is a global network of chief executives and business leaders who share the common bond of business success before the age of forty-five. Founded in 1950, the organization has more than 22,000 members in more than 125 countries. Chris had previously brought his YPO forum group of eight company presidents to build a Home of Hope. This was the only business group we had ever hosted, and they loved the hands-on opportunity to serve the poor. Chris's new idea to have us show our work to more members of YPO would soon affect our growth as a mission in unexpected ways.

The Vision and Values Conference had planned various off-site activities for the members during the afternoons. These included riding in a US nuclear submarine and playing golf at Torrey Pines, where the PGA holds events. When Chris proposed the idea of hosting a Homes of Hope tour in Mexico as one of their off-site options, Janet and I thought most would prefer to golf or ride a nuclear submarine rather than take a tour to see poor people. I told Chris we had room for up to thirteen people, and Janet made sure the van was clean and ready to go.

On the day of the tour, we were surprised to find sixteen people ready to be squished into our fifteen-passenger van! I drove while Janet rode in the back seat with two couples from Calgary, Canada—Helen and Kevin Jenkins and Jill and Robert Kulhawy. To our surprise, they were already aware of Homes of Hope. The children in both of their families had built a Home of Hope with their school. Robert explained that he had signed up for the nuclear submarine tour, but when they discovered he was a Canadian citizen, the US Navy considered him a security risk and wouldn't let him aboard! Robert was slightly annoyed, but being a good sport, he had jumped into the van to join his wife for the Homes of Hope tour.

Our plan was to first travel to a new *colonia* to visit a family who had recently received a Home of Hope. Then we would distribute some bags of rice and beans to needy families in the area. One of our staff members, Josue, had arranged for us to tour the newly built home. The family graciously allowed our group in, and we viewed each room to observe how the house was constructed. The mother of the family suffered from childhood polio and still walked with a limp, but her personality was vibrant and cheerful. She seemed to enjoy answering the group's questions. Although her husband was there, the poor guy could barely get a word in! She recalled her excitement upon learning that Homes of Hope was coming to build for her family.

"My husband was nervous about tearing down our old place to make room for the new construction. He said, 'What if they change their mind and don't build for us after all?' I tried to reassure him, but he was stubborn. 'I'm not going to help you tear down our house,' he told me. So I said, 'Well, I'm not going to cook for you and feed you anymore.'" She winked at her husband. "He eventually got hungry, and I won the argument!"

Everyone laughed as she continued her story. When she was done, I asked if there were any follow-up questions. I could sense that one of the members in the tour group was skeptical of what we were doing. He may have thought our organization was using the gift of a new home to pressure people into becoming Christians.

"What did they make you believe in order to get a house?" he asked.

The woman smiled. "My neighbors asked me the same question, and I told them they didn't make me believe anything. They only told me that God loved me and they loved me and wanted to serve my family in our time of need."

Satisfied by her answer, he nodded in agreement. What she was saying was true. We offer our Homes of Hope free of charge, provided the family receiving the house owns the land and meets the other basic criteria. No strings attached.

Next, someone asked the wife what she liked best about her new house. She paused and tears welled up in her eyes. "Before our family received this home, the only roof we had over our heads was a blue tarp. It filled up with water when it rained and often collapsed, soaking all of our belongings. I tried to put pictures of my children on the wall, but the storms ruined them."

She took a moment to compose herself, and another smile appeared on her face. "What I love most about my new house is that now when it rains, it's only wet on the outside."

I stood in the back by the window with tears streaming down my face. Her family had struggled against the elements for years, but after receiving a Home of Hope, they didn't need to worry about their belongings getting wet and destroyed any longer. They could shift their focus to more important issues in their lives.

After the house tour, we said our good-byes and made our way over to the food distribution area Josue had set up. A big crowd had gathered outside while we had been visiting with the family. We had enough food bags for two hundred people, and we were shocked to find almost six hundred waiting in line for food! We quickly broke down the supplies into smaller portions to make sure everyone came away with something to eat. Despite such a large crowd, the food distribution went off without a hitch.

During the return trip home, I glanced up at the rearview mirror and saw Janet engaged in deep conversation with the Kulhawys and the Jenkinses in the back of the van. She later told me that Helen had been calling different mission agencies in the hope of scheduling a mission trip for her whole family, but none of the agencies could accommodate her request.

Helen told Janet, "We have three kids. There's a mission trip that Kevin and I can go on as adults, or we can send the kids with the youth group at church. But we can't find a trip that we can go on together as a family."

In that moment a lightbulb went on for Janet as she caught Helen's passion to serve the poor with her whole family. Janet responded, "I think your three children are about the same age as ours, so why don't we bring our kids along and all build a Home of Hope together?"

Questions like this had motivated us so often in our ministry. God had asked us if we were willing to mobilize waves of young people, and we said yes. Our brother-in-law, Charlie, had asked us if we could arrange a mission trip for his whole youth group, and we said yes. My daughter Andrea had asked if I was going to build a house for the bus people, and we did. Now Helen was posing yet another question for us.

When you possess the heart of a servant, you're willing to move off of your own agenda and onto someone else's. The best businesses in the world operate on the same core servant principle—they are successful because they truly serve the needs of their customers.

Jill and Robert Kulhawy were also part of the conversation. They thought Homes of Hope could be a great activity for their family too and offered to join in on the trip. By the time the van arrived back at the hotel, a plan was in motion to have our three families build a Home of Hope between Christmas and New Year's. We had built hundreds of homes with high school youth, so why not with families? What could be better than families banding together to help another family in need?

Being a successful entrepreneur and strong visionary leader, Robert was seeing something bigger than the rest of us. A few hours later during dinner, he stood up in front of two hundred people and announced the YPO Fellowship Forum house build trip and welcomed other YPO families to join in. As a result, fourteen families (seventy people) signed up. It was remarkable that an idea initiated in the back of a crowded van could catch on so quickly. Instead of building one home for a family in need, we now would have the ability and personnel to do three.

MATTERS OF LIFE AND DEATH   89

Janet and I were thankful these business leaders were wanting to join us, but at the same time we were intimidated by the idea of hosting a bunch of successful business leaders and their families. Up until that point, we had only hosted high school kids. These young people didn't expect much in the way of amenities, and of course we did not charge them much either. I wasn't sure how these business executives and their families would react to the rough environment of the *colonias* or if our YWAM program services would meet their expectations. My uncertainty was soon dispelled as we worked out all the details of the trip. They were willing to pay a bit extra for their food, housing, and transportation, which in turn enabled us to provide upgraded food and more comfortable accommodations than our triple-high dorm room bunk beds.

When the families arrived, we did our normal Homes of Hope orientation and then loaded them into vans to go out to the work sites. We would be building homes for three families living in hillside shacks near Tijuana. Upon our arrival, our joyful mood quickly changed. One of the three homes we were building was for Pablo and Maria Ramirez and their seven children. When we walked up to meet them, it was obvious to everyone that they were extremely poor. They had dug into the side of the hill and put a big blue tarp over the top of the hole in the ground to protect them from the elements. All nine of them were living in this cave-like dwelling. Being exposed to such a scene was a moment of instant recalibration for everyone, including me. Before us was a family fighting simply to stay alive.

When the couple shuffled over to greet our group, Pablo reached out to shake our hands with a faint smile. Speaking through an interpreter, Pablo explained that two weeks earlier his six-month-old child had died from exposure. The revelation was like a punch in the gut. We had arrived to help his family feeling like we were all heroes, but we were two weeks late. If we had come to help them only a few weeks sooner, their baby might still have been alive. The only photo of the baby that Maria and Pablo had was the one our YWAM staff member had taken to create their family profile to share with the team before their arrival. They were grateful for this one memory of their young son.

Driving away from our build site that first day, I knew each member of our group was affected by what they had seen and done. Poverty is a lack of options, and this family had very few of them. The other two families we were building for had compelling stories as well, but not as tragic as that of the Ramirez family. The collective focus of our group turned a bit more serious as everyone began to grasp what was at stake. One thing remains a constant at the Homes of Hope build sites: you can never fully prepare yourself or predict the intensity of the situation you are entering into. On that day, our presence and work was a matter of life and death.

The media tends to paint the generic picture that all business leaders care about are profits and themselves. However, I was impressed by all the families I met. They were humble, caring, and willing to give of what they had to others. One of the men I connected with while building for the Ramirez family was Mike Regan from Chicago. When Mike and I had a chance to talk near the end of the first day, he turned to me with a thoughtful expression.

"You know, Sean, I'm a lot more like Pablo than I first thought. When I saw how he was living, I was immediately thankful to God for all the material blessings I had, but then it hit me that I have some significant spiritual poverty I need to deal with." Mike paused for a moment, the emotion building in his voice. "Pablo and I are both poor, just in different ways. God has so much more he wants to give me, but I am content to live under a blue tarp in my own spiritual poverty." We had all showed up to change the poor, but the poor were changing us.

The second day of building went well, as did the house dedications of all three new homes. As always, there were plenty of tears and hugs. Back at the hotel at the end of the day, we gathered everyone in a big circle for group sharing and debriefing. The response was overwhelmingly positive. Mike Regan's thirteen-year-old son, Patrick, had been reluctant to attend the trip as he preferred their normal family ski trip during Christmas break. Mike later told me that in the airport lounge on the way home, Patrick turned to him and said, "Dad, this is the best vacation we've ever had as a family."

Robert and Jill, the co-chairs of the event, conducted a survey of everyone who had participated, and the feedback was outstanding. Almost everyone from this first trip wanted to come back and was asking for next year's dates before Robert and I had even had a chance to talk about a second trip. Robert was bursting with new ideas for how to make the next trip even better. All the positive feedback meant a great deal to Janet and me.

The Homes of Hope experience was not only a reality check for the parents; they also saw it as an opportunity to educate their children about the world and to teach generosity and servanthood. One of the most consistent comments we hear back from families is that Homes of Hope helped recalibrate their whole family and provided them with a better perspective on life. It was clear now that families and business teams were going to play a part in our future growth.

TWELVE

VIPs

"The trouble is that rich people . . . very often don't really know who
the poor are; and that is why we can forgive them, for knowledge can
only lead to love, and love to service. And so, if they are not touched
by them, it's because they do not know them."

Mother Teresa

SOON after the first family group departed, we began hearing from
other YPO chapters that wanted information about bringing a group
on a Homes of Hope trip. Mike Regan had inspired his chapter in Chicago to join us, and Robert and Jill Kulhawy were promoting more
events as well. Robert and I often joked about how he was a security
risk and wondered what our lives would have been like had he been
allowed to ride in the nuclear submarine and missed the now-famous
Homes of Hope tour.

As we continued to host more business teams, Robert worked with
me to understand how to run better events. Before every event, we did
some creative planning sessions, during which Robert would often say,
"We need to dial this trip up." He had boundless energy and wanted us
to put on the best event possible.

The first few events were a challenge for our staff because our expertise was with high school youth. As we started "dialing up" the events, we added more food to our normally simple lunches and additional kinds of drinks at the work site. We also rented a portable toilet for every build site. We added some photography extras, and everyone got a group photo in a frame. We also made a music montage slide show to end every build.

Jill and Janet teamed up to add some housewarming gifts as part of each dedication ceremony. The housewarming gifts added a special touch and dignity to the dedication ceremony. Often the wife would burst into tears when she saw the new kitchen table set with matching plates and silverware. The children, upon entering the bedroom, would shout with glee, "Look, it's a real bed!" Eventually we standardized the "housewarming package" to include a kitchen table and chairs, a new stove, beds, curtains, and other basic household items. These were then delivered to the worksite on the second day just before the house dedication. The concept caught on with the youth house builds as well.

As the number of business teams increased, surprisingly so did the tension level among our staff. It seemed like we had two different kinds of participants. One was the youth groups who were happy with the lowest price and basic services, and the other was the business teams who were willing to pay more to have a nicer event. One day one of my senior leaders approached me and wanted to talk about our work with the business teams. As we sat together in my office, the leader pressed the view that we should only be working with church groups and youth, not rich people. With tears flowing, the leader said, "We are showing favoritism to the rich and preferring them over the church groups. We are ruining our witness with the Mexican churches and the pastors we are trying to serve."

The staff member quoted James 2 to me, which warns God's people not to show favoritism to rich people. "How can we take the business teams out to dinner and provide them with better food when we don't do the same for the youth teams? The rich get a portable toilet to use, while the youth are asked to use the neighbors' bathroom." I was stunned by all the emotion and the criticism being leveled at the business teams. The criticism did not feel right to me; it felt like misplaced judgment, but I wasn't sure how to reply. I said I would reflect on the issue and respond soon.

Were we showing favoritism to rich people? Janet and I had several discussions about the issue, and I talked with a few of our board members as well. I didn't want to be dismissive of the staff members' comments, but what they were implying didn't ring true to me.

The reality was that for more than a decade, Janet and I, along with our staff, had given 100 percent of ourselves to serve both the poor and the youth groups that came to serve. We worked long hours, and since most school breaks were in the spring and summer or around the holidays, we often deferred our vacation breaks to off periods of the year, sometimes sacrificing family events to serve the teams. Is it favoritism if one group is willing to pay extra to eat dinner at a Mexican restaurant and another group prefers to save that money and eat home-cooked spaghetti back at the dorms?

The more Janet and I talked, the more we realized the effort and energy we put forth to serve the youth groups and the business groups was exactly the same. If one group was willing to pay more to receive better food or stay at a hotel rather than in a dorm room, that didn't mean we were preferring them. At the end of the day, each group was choosing to pay for the options and level of service they desired. As staff, our commitment was to give our best efforts to serve both kinds of groups. The poor were the real VIPs!

Back in 1982 when I was sitting by the lake in Texas, God had called us to be servant leaders. We gave our best efforts to serve the poor, but we were also serving the youth, family, church, and business groups— whoever God sent to work with us.

After further discussions with our staff and board of directors, we formalized three different trip levels: Standard, Standard Plus, and Deluxe. Each visiting group could choose what level of experience they wanted. Our staff would give the same great effort to every group, no matter who they were or what level of service they chose.

One of the benefits of working with business teams was that our staff were forming wonderful relationships with many of their members. Many of these business partners began supporting our staff as well as giving to our ministry to help us grow. These men and women were skilled entrepreneurs who ran large and complex companies. Chris Crane had been a founding board member, and over time I invited other business leaders to join our board. When I first formed our nonprofit corporation in 1992, I simply tolerated the existence of the legal board. I saw it as a necessary evil and a requirement of the government so we could keep issuing tax-deductible receipts. As I matured in my leadership, I began to see the great value in having a strong board of directors to help oversee the ministry and properly steward all that God was giving us.

To help guide the growth of our board, we first looked for both men and women who had a deep faith in Christ. Although Homes of Hope was open to anyone who wanted to join us no matter what their faith or background was, it was a different story when it came to the board. We needed members who were willing to embrace our articles of incorporation and biblical worldview. Second, we sought members who loved and embraced YWAM's foundational values and core DNA. YWAM is a large and diverse movement, and as a ministry we often interact with YWAM operating locations and leaders from around the world. We needed board members who had a love for the whole mission. Third, we looked for board members who loved what we were doing locally in San Diego/Baja and were passionate about mobilizing groups to serve the poor and passionate about training and discipleship. Finally, we looked for board members whose talents and life skills fit our needs as a growing ministry.

One key individual that I brought onto our board was Dave Stone. We met Dave and his wife, Trina, during the first family build trip back in 1997. They were deeply touched by the Homes of Hope experience and quickly set a goal to participate in four home builds each year. In 1991 the Stones had started First Rate Inc., a software company located in Arlington, Texas. Dave and Trina ran the company with a distinct purpose. They had a call to missions just like Janet and I did, but they were expressing it through the sphere of business.

Steve James, who had been on an earlier build with Chris Crane, also agreed to join our board of directors. Steve is an astute business leader who has a gift for identifying and fixing organizational growth problems. We needed the wisdom of leaders like Steve to grow as an organization, but following their advice was sometimes a painful process for me. During our meetings, various members lovingly pointed out weaknesses in my leadership or organizational deficiencies that needed to be corrected.

After one of our board meetings, Steve said to me, "Sean, I love what you are doing, and I trust you. But you need to get YWAM San Diego/Baja formally audited on a regular basis."

"I know it's the right thing to do, Steve, but it's so time consuming and costs so much. That money could be used for other things to help grow the ministry in other ways."

"Trust me," Steve continued, "the audit will help us grow stronger. You owe it to your donors and to God to create a transparent financial process. I will keep bringing groups to build with you and contribute as a donor to YWAM, but I won't continue to serve on a nonprofit board that's unwilling to get audited."

Despite my apprehension about the cost and the huge amount of work needed to complete an audit, I accepted that it was the right thing to do to create ongoing financial stability and transparency. Everyone on the board rejoiced when the first audit report was completed. In the end, Steve was right. We learned a lot from the audit process, and the accompanying management letter had many helpful recommendations that made us better as an organization.

Having a rigorous board was not only benefiting our ministry; it was also helping me grow in my personal leadership. Having a compelling vision and good character is important, but so is having management skills that match the size and scope of the ministry you are leading. These mentors were helping me gain those skills.

Steve asked me if he could bring to Mexico a group of business leaders who were all part of a board he was on. He thought it would be good for them to participate in a Homes of Hope build because they had been going through a time of conflict about the future of their corporation. Steve said some were so frustrated they were threatening to sue one another. He also scheduled the company's next board meeting during the Home of Hope trip. It was a challenge to get all the members to come to Mexico, but at Steve's urging they agreed to the trip.

The first day of the build was dry and warm, and the board members got off to a good start. On this particular build, they were serving a young woman named Aurora who had three small children. Aurora's husband had recently left her, and although she owned land, she was living in a six-by-eight-foot wood structure with a tarp on top, held down by pallets. The next day, before the board members could finish the house, it started raining and didn't let up. The work site soon became awash in mud. By lunchtime everyone was wet, cold, muddy, and exhausted. The group wanted nothing more than to get back to the hotel to take hot showers and to rest. Steve decided that YWAM would need to finish the house at a later date when it stopped raining.

Steve slogged through the mud over to Aurora's shack to tell her and the children that someone else would finish her new home at a later date. When Steve opened the door, he noticed a river of water running through what used to be her dirt floor. Aurora was sitting on a makeshift bed holding her one-month-old child, shivering from the cold. In that moment, as Steve looked at her desperate living situation, he couldn't find the courage to tell Aurora the group was leaving. Instead, he smiled at her and said, "We are going to have lunch now, and then we will finish your new home." The young mother beamed a smile back to Steve as he closed the door.

Steve gathered his fellow board members together and informed them of the dire situation Aurora was facing. They all agreed to stick it out and finish the house. After the build, my staff told me it was one of the toughest house builds they had ever been a part of. But the team got the house done and handed the keys over to Aurora and her three children.

The next day, back at the hotel, Steve and the team gathered for their board meeting with a new attitude and perspective. During the meeting, they were able to resolve all of their differences and make decisions beneficial to the future of the company. Steve told me later, "Sean, it was amazing to see how Homes of Hope adjusted everyone's perspective. It was the best kind of team-building event and exactly what our board needed to get us back on track."

Our business group numbers continued to increase, but our staff numbers were not growing. The most staff we had at any one time was twenty-eight, and we couldn't manage to surpass that number. Within YWAM, there are two methods to increase staff numbers. You can develop your own by running an entry-level Discipleship Training School (DTS), or you can recruit staff that have been trained by another YWAM campus. I chose the latter option. It was a lot of work to establish and run a DTS, as it took a real focus of leadership and extra staff, and the students would have used up campus housing and other resources that could be used for our teams.

I had reasoned that we would let other YWAM centers run the DTS training while we focused on running our youth and Homes of Hope programs. I was a good recruiter, and there were lots of YWAM centers running DTS programs, so I figured I would eventually find enough free agents to build our staff numbers up. I would soon discover my thinking was flawed.

Fresh understanding came to me while attending a YWAM leaders gathering in Brazil with my coworker Joe Matta. Our international founder, Loren Cunningham, was one of the keynote speakers. Loren's topic was organizational growth and the importance of doing your own training.

"I've been studying organizational growth," Loren told the YWAM leaders, "and I've found that it's extremely difficult for nonprofit organizations to grow past thirty staff members unless they're intentional about their own training and staff development."

I sat in stunned silence as Loren delivered his message. The implications were clear—no intentionality in training equals no real growth. After hearing this, I looked at Joe and whispered, "I guess we need to start doing our own DTS right away." Joe nodded in agreement. Upon our return to Baja, we immediately made plans to run a DTS. It would be a lot of work, but I was willing to pay the price to have healthy, fruitful growth.[1]

Our Tijuana center was always full, and we needed to consider other accommodation options for our groups. One of our newer staff members, Sandra Williams, loved to take teams down to the city of Ensenada, about an hour's drive south on a toll road that has magnificent views of the Pacific Ocean. At first glance, Ensenada feels like a sleepy beach town, but it is bigger than it looks, with a population of almost half a million. There are many foreign factories and farms on the edges of the

1. To find out more about the DTS program, go to www.ywamsandiegobaja.org/dts.

city, and thousands of poor families live in the same squalid housing conditions that I had first seen with Sergio in El Florido.

Sandra asked me if we could start running our spring and summer Mission Adventures youth programs in Ensenada. Andy Ortega, who had joined our staff a few years earlier, was familiar with the area and offered to help Sandra organize everything. We soon rented housing for our teams and made great connections with local churches and orphanages.

Sandra possessed great enthusiasm for our youth programs, which flourished under her leadership. One day she urged me to come to Ensenada to show me a building she thought would be a great fit for a new YWAM center. I met her on the south side of Ensenada. The building was a failed condominium project that had been sitting empty for six years.

As we stood in front of the building, Sandra turned to me and said, "Sean, you need to buy this building for YWAM."

"Buy it with what?" I asked, smiling. "We don't have any money to invest in a building like this, plus the cost of the renovations will be high."

Sandra didn't waver. "Will you at least pray about it?"

"Yes, I will pray about it."

Over the next few months, we did pray. And the more we prayed, the more it seemed like a perfect building for our growing work in Ensenada. Joe researched the property, and our Mexican attorney, Rodolfo, became involved in the process. Joe and I did some calculations and realized that with all the teams we were hosting in Ensenada, lots of money was already being spent on high-cost rental situations. It was clear these funds could be used to make a monthly payment on the building, if the owner was willing to carry the loan.

Joe and I worked together to create a seven-year purchase proposal. Our down payment would be low because we needed funds to execute much-needed renovations. We committed to make seven annual balloon payments and pay $2,500 a month in rent until we had completed the final balloon payment. To our surprise, the owner agreed to our small down payment and to carry the full note. It gave him the assurance that if we failed to complete our payment plan, he would get his property back and benefit from all our improvements and upgrades.

We were now running multiple DTS schools a year, and as Loren predicted, our staff numbers started to grow. We had virtually outgrown our original property in Playas, adding several rental buildings in the area to deal with all the growth. For more than a decade, we had hosted thousands of youth each year in our small but functional six-thousand-square-foot building. We were landlocked and had no further room to grow or expand in the Playas area.

By the end of 2000 we were building over 160 houses per year in Baja. Most of the business teams coming to Tijuana were opting to stay in nearby hotels, rather than sleeping in our crowded dorm rooms with triple-high bunk beds. The Ensenada campus had many smaller rooms, each with its own bathroom, and a giant courtyard where everyone could hang out. Our teams enjoyed staying there.

The Mission Adventures youth programs in Ensenada soon grew so large that we had to do our group sessions outside in an empty lot with a big covered stage. At night we often had a worship band play with a big, loud sound system. The youth loved it. What we didn't realize initially was that our neighbors didn't. The sound from our worship band carried for blocks in all directions. Several neighbors started a petition to get us kicked off the property. Once we discovered what was going on, we worked to address the issue, enclosing the outdoor area and making it soundproof. Despite our efforts, a number of months later we received a formal notice that the city council was going to do a site visit to assess whether or not we should be removed from the neighborhood.

On the day the city council members arrived to audit us, everyone was uneasy because there was a real possibility we wouldn't be allowed to continue our work in Ensenada. Although I wasn't able to be present at the meeting, I asked our team to make sure we conveyed to the city council everything we were doing to remedy the noise situation and also stress the importance of the work we were doing with Homes of Hope. Our staff was in the middle of their presentation when one of the council members suddenly stopped the meeting.

"Can I please speak?" he asked.

Our team was eager to accommodate, so the councilman continued. "I have this friend. His marriage was struggling because he didn't have a job. He was a poor provider, and there was a lot of stress in his marriage. His kids weren't happy, and his young children were living in a house made of old pieces of wood. My friend was depressed and about to give up on life. And then my friend got one of your Homes of Hope, and it changed his life."

The man suddenly became emotional and blurted out, "My name is Humberto, and I am that friend! I received one of your homes many years ago, and it changed my life. And as you can see, I am now here on the Ensenada City Council."

Needless to say, we didn't get shut down and kicked out of the neighborhood!

I was encouraged by the growth we were experiencing at our Ensenada campus. Having our own facilities that we could customize and develop long-term was a huge blessing.[2] At our Playas center in Tijuana, however, I was growing more frustrated every day with our facilities or lack thereof. We did not have enough parking or storage, our kitchen was too small, our team housing was laughable, we did not have enough office work space, and as a result, it was becoming difficult to retain long-term staff.

In my travels around Tijuana I would often stop and look at properties with For Sale signs, but nothing ever came of these random searches. Pastor Abel, who led a church in the Playas area, had offered to sell us some land his church owned in another part of the city. I went to look at it, but it was not a good fit for our uses, and we still had no money to buy property. To keep growing, we would need some kind of property breakthrough in Tijuana orchestrated by God, like we had experienced in Ensenada just a few years prior.

2. To see a short video of the Ensenada campus, go to www.ywamsandiegobaja.org/locations/.

THIRTEEN

Inheritance in the Land

"The boundary lines have fallen for me in pleasant places;
surely I have a delightful inheritance."

Psalm 16:6

WHEN Janet and I were on staff at YWAM Los Angeles, John Dawson had a habit of saying in our staff meetings, "The boundary lines have fallen for me in pleasant places; surely I have a delightful inheritance." John quoted that verse from Psalm 16 so often that it has stuck in my head to this day. God had already provided a home for us in San Diego in 1995, and in 1998 YWAM had been able to purchase a beautiful property in Ensenada. However, in Tijuana, where so much of our work was centered, we possessed no real inheritance. The possibility of ever owning property in the Tijuana area was highly unlikely, unless we came upon a miracle. And that is exactly what happened.

In 2000 I received a phone call from a businessman and his wife, who said they wanted to meet with Janet and me. We set up a time to visit them at their home. We gathered around a small table, and the husband spoke first: "We like what you are doing with YWAM, and your work with the poor has touched us. Recently, we were able to sell our company, and we set aside some funds from the sale of the company to give away."

I got excited as I started considering how much the gift could be. It was unlikely this couple would ask us to travel all the way to their home for $1,000 or even $10,000. In ten years as a ministry, the biggest gift the ministry had ever received was $25,000.

The husband continued to talk, occasionally looking down at his notes. "My wife and I have never given away a gift this large before, and we are blessed to be able to tell you that we would like to give YWAM San Diego/Baja one million dollars to buy land in Mexico to establish a YWAM campus."

I was so shocked I couldn't do anything except take a deep breath and lean back in my chair to let it all sink in. I looked over at Janet and smiled. We had never asked this couple to give money for land in Mexico. We had never handed them a brochure or shown them a PowerPoint presentation. God had touched their hearts to give to YWAM so we could have an inheritance of land in Tijuana.

As the conversation continued, the wife said that if we accepted the million-dollar gift, we had to agree to never go into debt to buy land or build any future facilities. They were thoughtful in their giving and did not want the campus to be put at risk by future borrowing. We have since expressed gratitude to God countless times for the wisdom that accompanied this gift.

As Janet and I traveled home, my mind was spinning. What was in the mind of God that he would give us this kind of money to steward? No matter the answer, God was definitely up to something big. I also knew it was going to be a challenge to find the right property in Tijuana to fit our ministry needs.

Over the next few months, I checked out several Tijuana area locations until I discovered one five-acre property that looked promising. The strong point of the property was its location; it was just off one of the main roads between Tijuana and Rosarito, which would allow us easy access to anywhere in the city. The price tag was $600,000, so that would leave us $400,000 to put up our first building. I asked a few board members and some senior staff to go with me to look at the land. As everyone exited the van, I began sharing my vision for the property and its development and why I thought it was an ideal fit for YWAM. There was a sharp contrast between my overflowing enthusiasm about the property and the sour expressions on everyone's faces.

Drew Smith, one of our board members, finally spoke up. "What about all of the goats?" he asked.

"Goats? I don't see any goats," I answered.

"You don't need to see them. Can't you *smell* them?"

I took a moment to sniff the air, and that's when the stench hit me for the first time. Drew walked me over to the edge of the property and pointed into an adjacent lot where hundreds of goats were penned up. I had been so excited about the property that I hadn't noticed the goats. I felt silly at first, but I also learned a big lesson that day. As a visionary leader, you have to be careful not to get too fixated on any one solution. If you do, you can lose your objectivity and miss something that should be obvious—like goats!

It was more difficult than I thought to identify the right property, so I asked Steve James and Chris Crane for assistance. They helped me create a real-estate grid to rank the attributes of each location I was considering. We developed criteria such as location, parking, space for future buildings, and long-term growth potential and then assigned each criteria a numeric score. Every property I looked at had different attributes, but above all I wanted a property we could grow into, not one we would quickly grow out of.

One day Janet and I were driving from Playas down to our Ensenada campus when she was reminded of a KOA campground she had stayed at back in 1977 as a nineteen-year-old participating in the YWAM Bibles for Mexico outreach. The campground was located in a community called San Antonio del Mar, just off the toll road.

Janet turned to me as we were getting close to the property: "We should go see if that old campground is for sale, because it would be perfect for a YWAM campus."

Without giving it another thought, I drove up to the campground. It was perched on a hill with beautiful views of the Pacific Ocean. Janet was right—this would make a great property for our new YWAM campus. I had spent months looking at countless properties, and none of them were a good fit, but this property had great potential. It was not only an ideal location but also the perfect size to give us room for future growth.

We located the property manager in the only building there and asked if the land was for sale. To my surprise, the older man nodded his head. He said it was owned by a tobacco company from Tepic, Mexico, that was asking *two* million dollars for the property. He provided us with the contact information for the owners, and we thanked him for his time. This property ranked extremely high on our numeric grid. However, the two-million-dollar price tag was way above what we could afford. Janet and I prayed together for God's will to be made known to us and for him to guide us if this property was our inheritance.

A few days later I tracked down the owners of the land. Chris Crane had taught me that "cash is king." So I offered a one-million-dollar, all-cash offer for the land, hoping for a quick sale over the phone. The owners politely rejected my offer. Although I was disappointed, there was nothing more I could do. My only option was to continue searching for properties in our price range.

Nine months later the owners of the KOA campground called me. They said they were lowering the price to one and a half million dollars. A spark of hope filled my heart. I had looked at lots of properties, and none were as perfect as this one. Over the last few months I had been able to get some additional donations. Along with some cash reserves we had, I thought we might be able to come up with $1.2 million, but that still put us $300,000 short. Despite our limited cash position, I was still excited about the price reduction. I went to our board with the news and proposed we enter into negotiations with the owners.

Once again, Steve James was there to offer some crucial advice before we moved forward.

"I would never vote in favor of buying a property that big without getting both a geological and an environmental study done, because it's important that we know what we're buying," Steve told the board.

"Steve, those studies will probably cost around $35,000," I said, pushing back on his idea. "What are we going to learn about the property for that price? After all, it's just a campground."

Steve wasn't budging. "Sean, no matter how great the deals may be, I'm not voting to buy anything this big without having all the right information."

Deep down, I knew Steve wanted what was best for our ministry. He had wisely guided us years ago to get our financial house in order, and it seemed highly unlikely that we would have received the million-dollar gift without a consistent auditing process in place. Although I hated spending the money, I agreed to get both studies done.

I had asked Chris to lead the negotiations with the owners while I would try to generate more prayer and money. But Chris suggested I take a more active role in the negotiation process. One night he called me at home with an idea.

"Listen, Sean, there is a two-day class on negotiating I think you should attend. It costs $800, but you can bring a second person for free. I would be happy to pay for it if you would go."

A negotiations class? I mused to myself. That didn't sound interesting to me at all. I was a missions guy—what did I need to know about negotiations?

"Thanks for the kind offer, Chris, but you're the Harvard business guy. You're doing the negotiations," I told him. "I'm the prayer guy, remember? I don't have much interest in going to a class on negotiations."

I politely declined Chris's offer, but he was persistent, *very* persistent. I dreaded the thought of spending two full days listening to a lecture on negotiating. With all my other leadership duties, my schedule was already full. Yet out of respect for our friendship, I called him back and grudgingly agreed to attend the class.

I had a bad attitude as I walked into the class the first day. I would rather have gone to the dentist to get a root canal than listen to some boring teacher rattle on about something in which I had no interest. To my surprise, the class was remarkably interesting and informative. On the second day, a convergence happened in my brain, and I came out of the class with several negotiation strategies that I knew would help in the purchasing of the new property.

Just as Steve had predicted, when the results of the environmental and geological studies came back, we learned valuable information about the San Antonio Del Mar property. There was an uncontained diesel tank on the property and the septic field for the campground had broken down. There was also a problem with an electrical transformer leaking some PCB (polychlorinated biphenyl) chemicals. All these issues were solvable, but they did diminish the value of the property. The geological study revealed minor fault lines that would affect where we could erect future buildings.

By the time we went in to negotiate with the owners, we knew more about their property than they did. Inspired by the negotiating class, I developed a strategy to engage the owners. Chris continued to be our primary spokesman, and my primary role was to be the "good news guy," sharing all about what our organization was doing to help the poor. Joe would give a report on the environmental and geological issues we had discovered, so he would act as the "bad news guy."

After a few hours of friendly negotiations, the owners agreed to sell us the campground for $1,275,000. We were now the proud owners of a twelve-acre property overlooking the Pacific Ocean. By taking the negotiating class and getting the land studies done, we saved YWAM San Diego/Baja $225,000!

Our next step was to focus on how to develop the property and keep it all debt-free. San Diego architects Doug Austin and Eduardo Savigliano agreed to take on the master planning for the property free of charge. Meanwhile, Brett and Karen Curtis joined our senior leadership team. Brett would serve as our overall operations director, and Karen agreed to help in our development department. God kept sending the right people at the right time to help us grow. Brett, Joe, and I put together a scope document that outlined the future vision for the full development of the property. In the ninety-page document, we listed the programs we envisioned running on the campus and how many staff it would take to run them. Lastly, we built a cash flow projection model looking at all the costs of running the new campus versus the income we would generate through our programming.

This document, combined with a professional master planning process, yielded an overall vision for the new property that was compelling. Once the property was fully developed, it would be an eight-hundred-bed facility with four distinct focuses or sections. One section would be dedicated to running youth programs, another section would be designed for families and business teams, another section would be for University of the Nations students, and the final area would be for staff housing. Although there were specific design elements for each section, it was important to have the campus be as interchangeable and flexible as possible, to allow for future growth in any area.

I was eager to charge ahead with construction on our new land, but things were going slowly. Two years had passed since we bought the property, and we still hadn't raised enough money to start the building process. One day I shared my growing frustration with Dean Sherman. Dean had been one of my favorite discipleship teachers years ago. I took him on a tour of the property and asked if he had any suggestions to see a breakthrough in getting more funding for the development.

Dean turned to me and said, "You know, the problem I see with many YWAM leaders is they don't have the right theology of faith."

"What do you mean?"

"You believe God is your provider, right?"

"Well, of course he is," I said.

Dean continued, becoming more passionate as he spoke. "Think about it this way. Joshua in the Old Testament knew he couldn't win the battle for the promised land without God, right? But God wouldn't simply *give* the land to Joshua and the people without them first picking up their swords, designing a battle plan, and then going out to fight and execute that plan."

I immediately connected with Dean's message. I realized I had grown a bit passive in my faith over the past two years since we got the unsolicited million-dollar gift.

"When did the people of Israel see miracles?" Dean continued, looking me in the eyes. "It was when they put one foot before the other with their sword in their hand and went forward to contend for the land. It was only when they engaged in the battle that God performed miracles."

A new level of faith was rising in me.

"Here is my point, Sean. God wants to do it with you, not for you. We serve a relational God. Don't be presumptuous. Get the right battle plan, but then go out and communicate your vision to others. It will be while you're communicating your vision and in the midst of the battle that you will see God do the miracles you're longing to see."

Dean's message was the exact encouragement I needed. The process he was describing was precisely what had happened to me in 1979 when

I joined YWAM. Each time God spoke to me, it was as I took a step of obedience that I saw a corresponding release of the resources I needed. It was my role to communicate our vision as a ministry and invite people to join us. It was God's job to touch hearts about what they were to give or how they were to be involved with us.

After I met with Dean, Chris Crane connected me with Bob Westfall. Bob had worked with Walk Thru the Bible for many years and then started his own company to help mentor nonprofit leaders in how to resource their ministries. Bob helped me pull together a major donor event called The President's Gathering. This was a vision weekend during which I, as president of YWAM San Diego/Baja, invited businesspeople and their families to join us for a weekend of building homes for the poor and finding out more about our ministry. Near the end of the weekend I would ask attendees to consider giving to our vision. We placed a large punch bowl in the back of the room and invited people to respond as God led them. No high-pressure sales pitch, no begging, only an invitation to join us in resourcing the vision at whatever level they felt comfortable.

During one of our President's Gathering weekends, I met with a couple who had recently sold their company. I enthusiastically presented our vision and handed them a half sheet of paper listing our phase-one construction goals. Our immediate need was to raise $1.8 million to get the basic infrastructure in and then start the vertical construction process. During our conversation I considered asking them to give $100,000, but I decided not to and just let God speak to them however he wanted. The next day we met again, and they informed me that they intended to give the full $1.8 million needed for phase one! I never could have imagined them giving such a large amount. This was just the breakthrough we had been praying for.

At the next President's event, however, I forgot the wisdom of letting God prompt the giving, and I asked a businessman for a specific gift of $45,000. I thought this was a nice number as he had given in the past, and I knew he liked what we did. I was surprised when he informed me that he was not happy with me asking for such a big number. He wondered how I could possibly know if he had $45,000 lying around in the bank to give to YWAM. I apologized for my bold presumption, and he accepted my apology. He still graciously gave a gift, just not $45,000. He gave what he felt comfortable giving, not what I thought he should give.

What I learned from these two situations is that it's okay to know your own numbers as a ministry, but it's not appropriate to project your needs onto someone else. Giving typically is a private matter between God and the donor. I have found that having the right theology about giving and receiving is important. It makes me relaxed and full of faith as a leader. I know my role is to get better and better at sharing our ministry vision with others, and it is God's job to touch hearts about what to give. As Bob Westfall often says, "We only have one donor, and that is God."

With funding to start phase one in place, once again Chris Crane played a vital role in helping YWAM San Diego/Baja advance our vision. Chris connected me with Tom Wermers, who ran a large development and construction company. Tom wanted to give back beyond writing a check and offered not only to join our YWAM board but also to chair our board property committee. Tom's expertise and leadership were an invaluable contribution as we put the infrastructure in and started to go vertical with our new buildings. We also added Kevin Callaway to our team as the overall project manager. Kevin and I had served together on staff in LA back in the 1980s. Kevin was fluent in Spanish and had a degree in project management. Pat Eachus would eventually join the property committee as well, helping with all the design elements of each new building.

All of the key elements and pieces were coming together like a jigsaw puzzle—we owned twelve acres of debt-free land overlooking the Pacific Ocean, and God was providing us with all the right people to steward well all the resources God was sending our way.[1] The boundary lines were falling for us in pleasant places, and our inheritance in the land was delightful.

1. To see a short video of the San Antonio del Mar campus, go to www.ywamsandiegobaja.org/locations/.

FOURTEEN

An Idol No More

"Those who cling to worthless idols turn away from God's love for them."

Jonah 2:8

JANET and I had both given up our university educations to become missionaries with YWAM. I had never been a great student, so leaving school was not a hard choice for me, but it was for Janet. She had been valedictorian of her high school class and had gone on to attend Portland State University in Oregon. After one year, she pushed the pause button on her formal education to attend a DTS in Los Angeles, followed by an outreach to La Paz in southern Baja. She followed God's leading and never looked back, but her decision was more painful than I knew.

During our engagement, we would often have long conversations at the Sunland house where Janet lived or over coffee at the nearby Bob's Big Boy Restaurant. One of those conversations opened my eyes to just how significant education had been to her.

"Sean, I know your story of dropping out of college to join YWAM. Let me tell you mine." Janet paused to take a sip of coffee. "My dad wanted six sons, but he got five daughters and only one son. I was the youngest of the six, and I don't remember getting much if any affirmation or encouragement from my dad. He grew up in a poor family during the Depression era, and he was very intelligent, but school was a struggle for him. I did well in school, so well that I got a lot of attention there. Eventually education became an idol in my life."

I interrupted Janet, "I thought an idol was some kind of big statue of a mythical creature that you bow down and worship. How can something good like education be an idol?"

"An idol can be anything in our lives that we start living for or draw strength from or find our identity in, other than God himself."

"That's a powerful definition."

"For some people their idol is money or public recognition in their career; for me education was an idol. The more I succeeded in school, the more I found my identity and self-worth had become wrapped up in my educational success. While in La Paz I had this transformational prayer time."

"What happened? Why was it transformational?" I asked.

"I finally realized my self-worth was wrapped up in my educational success and not in God himself. In that moment I chose to find life and joy in God alone and to stop striving for my educational success. It was one of the most freeing moments of my life."

Now many years later our oldest daughter, Rachel, was graduating from high school and wanted to attend Point Loma Nazarene University. Although I was happy to see my daughter going on to college, I was nervous about our ability to pay for her tuition. As Janet and I were filling out all the paperwork and financial aid forms, everything seemed overwhelming to me. Rachel was going to need money for tuition, room and board, books, and living expenses. I had no idea where these funds were going to come from. I was squawking about every form we had to fill out and all the money we were going to have to spend. Finally Janet had enough of my negativity.

"It does not take two of us to fill out this paperwork, Sean," Janet vented. "You're driving me crazy! Go do something else, and I will finish all of the forms."

Janet later took a break from the paperwork and left to do some grocery shopping. As she was turning into the Costco parking lot, God clearly spoke to her. It was not an audible voice but a clear message that came into her mind and filled her with inner peace: *You and Sean gave up your education for me, and now I'm going to give it back to your children.*

Rachel was a straight-A student and was accepted into Point Loma. Thankfully she also qualified for a number of scholarships, but even with the help of the scholarships, Rachel had to take out some student loans. In later years we took on parent loans to help her.

About halfway through her senior year, Rachel began to think about serving with YWAM after she graduated. But the student loans were a growing concern for her as she neared graduation. While Janet and Rachel were walking through our neighborhood during her Christmas break, Rachel brought up the subject.

"Mom, what if I want to join YWAM after college?" she asked. "How will I ever pay these loans off?"

Janet encouraged Rachel not to worry. "God has always taken care of our family. If God wants you in YWAM, then God will help you to pay off the loans."

As we had done so many times before in our lives, we prayed and left the situation in God's hands. After nearly four years of private university education, we would end up with about $40,000 worth of parent and student loans.

A few months before Rachel was to graduate, our family completed a Homes of Hope build along with Larry and Judy Moon. The Moons were friends from Wisconsin and had children around the same ages as our daughters. After the build, they planned to stay a few extra days in San Diego. When Janet heard this, she invited them over to our house to celebrate Andrea's birthday, which is December 31, New Year's Eve. Together our families had a blast ringing in 2005.

The next morning I received an unexpected phone call from Larry, explaining it was important for Janet and me to join him and Judy for coffee at their hotel. Truthfully, I felt a bit uneasy after hanging up from our call. Our families had just spent four wonderful days together, but I began to wonder if we or one of our staff had offended them in some way. It had to be something serious if Larry did not feel comfortable telling me on the phone.

When we sat down with the Moons at their hotel, Larry's smile instantly disarmed my fears. "Listen, Judy and I have been talking, and we thought about adopting you two and supporting you as missionaries . . . but we realize you both are a little too old for that," Larry said with a laugh. "We have talked this over, and we want to adopt your daughters' education. They are free to choose whatever school they want to attend and whatever courses they wish to study. They will not be required to show us their grades, but they need to complete the work. We believe in education and love giving to it."

As the reality of what was being communicated slowly sank in, Janet and I were both overcome with emotion. The word God had spoken to Janet in the Costco parking lot was being fulfilled in a very tangible way. Larry and Judy's gift made us feel like we had just won the lottery, only this was better because we knew it was a gift prompted by our generous Father in heaven. Larry and Judy told us they were going to pay off the remaining balance on all of Rachel's student loans. She now would graduate debt-free! It was a huge relief because I had seen debt limit so many young people's choices to go into the ministry.

When we returned home from meeting with Larry and Judy, we couldn't wait to tell our girls the amazing news. At the time, Andrea was a senior in high school. Ever since she was a young girl, she had told everyone, "I want to be a missionary when I grow up." Andrea also had a dream to go to university, and now that would be paid for by the generosity of the Moon family. The Moons also told us that we could put our youngest daughter, Tiffany, into a quality private high school, which they would pay for as well. Together we all began praising God for this amazing provision.

The next day was Sunday, and we all went to our home church at Faith Chapel. Andrea went to the youth group service, and Janet and I attended the main adult service. When we met up with each other after church, Andrea bounced toward us with a glowing smile.

"You won't believe what happened in youth church today. They passed out letters we had written to God one year ago. In my letter I had asked God to provide for me to go to university so I could graduate debt-free and become a missionary. I had forgotten I had even written that letter!"

God was fulfilling his promise to Janet and me by giving education back to our children and answering Andrea's prayer so she could fulfill her dream to be a missionary. It was a true miracle. Andrea chose to attend Trinity Western University in British Columbia, Canada.

Homes of Hope had completed our one thousandth home build in 2002, and by 2007 we were approaching the two thousandth home. To commemorate the achievement, I thought it would be fitting to capture the two thousandth home build with a video story. As I scanned the Homes of Hope calendar, I noticed there were three teams scheduled to build on the weekend we would complete this home. As I stared closer at the calendar, I noticed one of the three teams was being led by Andrea. While attending Trinity Western University, she had gotten involved in New Beginnings, a youth ministry in Vancouver. New Beginnings was made up of a large number of First Nations youth. Andrea had inspired the second Home of Hope to be built in 1990, and seventeen years later she was still influencing others to build homes for those in need. It was only fitting that the video should be about the group she was bringing from Vancouver.

Andrea, who grew up interacting with the poor during our home builds around Tijuana, quickly became attached to the First Nations youth she met at New Beginnings. She saw how challenging life was for them in the inner city of Vancouver. Many native families were torn apart by domestic violence, alcoholism, drug abuse, and other painful social problems. They were in desperate need of good role models and people who believed in them.

One of the leaders of the New Beginnings youth group was a woman named Karla. She had reached out to Andrea because she had heard that Janet and I were missionaries in Mexico. Karla said she had always wanted to take the youth group on a mission trip and asked Andrea if she could help set one up. Andrea assured Karla she would get more information about doing a trip and offered to help her organize it. They discovered it would cost $30,000 for the entire group to travel to Mexico and pay for the building materials and program fees. Andrea and Karla organized the kids in a series of car washes and aluminum can drives. They also put together a profile for each youth and contacted donors to ask them to consider sponsoring one of them to go to

Mexico. One donor gave enough money to make sure all sixteen youth could go.

These youth, many of whom had never traveled beyond the inner city of Vancouver, still faced significant obstacles. For many of them it was a struggle to even get a passport. As minors, they needed permission from both parents to leave the country. Andrea spoke with one mother who said of her daughter's father, "I think I remember his name, but I don't know how to find him." The majority of the First Nations youth were considered youth at risk and came from extremely complicated family backgrounds. Andrea and Karla had managed to get them all to believe that they could travel down to Mexico and make a difference in the lives of others. There is something powerful about a trip that involves acts of giving rather than just getting.

As the youth group traveled to Mexico, they discovered that the Mission Adventures theme for the summer was "detox." In its broadest sense, this theme was meant to inspire youth to detox from the world in general and be filled with God's love and purpose. But for many of the Vancouver youth, the detox theme had additional meanings. Some had their own addictions to drugs or alcohol. Andrea marveled at how the kids came alive through serving. Something awakened in their spirits as they worked on the two thousandth Home of Hope and interacted with its recipients, Raymundo and Elena Lopez and their seven children.

Raymundo and Elena's family were also First Nations people from southern Mexico. They had relocated to the hills of Ensenada from the state of Oaxaca, one of the poorest states in Mexico. They had come to find work at one of the many foreign factories in the area. They eventually got some land, but they did not have enough money to build a proper home. So they formed a small structure out of plywood with a tarp roof and a dirt floor. Raymundo and Elena were making the best of their situation, but they were only earning around seventy dollars a week between the two of them. It was clear that before Homes of Hope entered the situation, there was little hope for them to envision a brighter future.

When the New Beginnings youth arrived, they had an immediate and deep connection with the Lopez family. There were plenty of smiles and abundant laughter out at the work site. Raymundo and Elena's youngest son, Joel, who was in third grade at the time, tried to help in various ways. When someone asked him what he wanted to be when he grew up, Joel answered, "I know I am going to be a very important person one day." His answers made the Vancouver crew want to do even more to support the family and make Joel's dreams come true.

Many of the New Beginnings youth remarked how the experience of building a Home of Hope had changed them. Desiree, who celebrated her sixteenth birthday on one of the build days, told everyone, "I got a lot of gifts today, but the greatest gift from God was just to be here to help these people. Just doing something for others even when you don't have much, you give what you do have and it feels so good. I think that this is the best summer, the best day, the best birthday, and the greatest part of my life . . . or the greatest part of the *beginning* of my life!"

Desiree had never had a stable home environment and had already experienced many hardships in her young life. She already had a young son of her own. In helping build a house for the Lopez family, Desiree felt for the first time in her life that she could make a difference in someone else's life. Back in Vancouver, she arranged for another youth group member to watch her son on Wednesday nights so she could volunteer at a local soup kitchen. Desiree served and helped feed the many homeless people who showed up at the kitchen, including her own mother, who often came through the food line.

After the Mexico build, Karla opened a group home where many of the kids could live until they were able to graduate from high school, which was a first in most of the families. Over the next few years, about a third of the New Beginnings youth from the initial trip graduated from high school and went on to college. Karla continues to partner with us and arrange youth trips to Mexico.

Several years later, Andrea and some of the New Beginnings team visited the Lopez family. Raymundo and Elena's children were excelling in school. A few of them had graduated from high school and were now taking college-level courses. Andrea said the Home of Hope they received had been turned into bedrooms for their seven children. They had since added on a bedroom for the parents and a large living room.

Maybe the most poignant moment came when the family invited Andrea inside and sat her down by their laptop computer. "What's your

Facebook name?" one of the daughters asked. After Andrea navigated them to her personal page, the girls "friended" her!

Around their property they had put in a wonderful garden full of plants and vegetables to help provide food for the family. Andrea told us Raymundo and Elena's situation reminded her of a Bible passage:

> The LORD will surely comfort Zion
>   and will look with compassion on all her ruins;
> he will make her deserts like Eden,
>   her wastelands like the garden of the LORD.
> (Isaiah 51:3)

Years earlier, this family had come to Ensenada with nothing. Since receiving a Home of Hope, they had turned their desert land into a garden of hope.[1]

---

1. To see a short video of the two thousandth home, go to www.ywamhomesofhope.org/2000.

FIFTEEN

The Perfect Storm

"Never be afraid to trust an unknown future to a known God."

Corrie ten Boom

IN 2007 we hosted 6,300 participants in various Baja programs and built 292 Homes of Hope for the poor—our biggest year ever. We anticipated even more consistent growth, but unforeseen nationwide crises in Mexico suddenly threatened all of our programs.

The president of Mexico at the time, Felipe Calderón, declared war on the drug cartels and arrested their key leaders, which ultimately created a vacuum of authority. This sparked a violent power struggle within the cartels and among the big three cartels to decide which would control the major drug routes into the United States.

Soon the news reports about the Mexico drug wars began to affect our incoming group numbers. In 2008 we hosted 4,975 people, a drop of 22 percent from the previous year. In early 2009 the US economy was crashing, even as the drug wars continued to escalate. The fighting among the cartels was so violent that the Mexican government sent in the military to help police set up checkpoints all around northern Baja. We never saw or experienced any of the violence or felt unsafe at any time while traveling around Baja. But anyone watching or reading the graphic news reports wouldn't have felt inspired to come to Mexico, and I couldn't blame them.

If that wasn't disheartening enough, in April 2009 we began to hear reports of an outbreak of the swine flu in southern Mexico. The president of Mexico ordered all the public schools and universities to shut down. Several major North American airlines stopped flying into the country. Many experts were predicting the outbreak was going to affect the whole world. Daily we were receiving calls from groups canceling their mission trips with us. They felt the environment was simply too unstable for them to risk traveling south of the border.

"What we have here is the perfect storm," Steve James told me when I sought his advice about how to guide our ministry through the crisis.

That same day, Janet was having her morning devotions and encountered the story in Mark 4 about Jesus and the disciples going across a lake in a boat. They were hit by a ferocious storm that sent the disciples into a panic. Where was Jesus during the storm? He was in the stern of the boat, peacefully asleep. When the disciples woke Jesus up, he rebuked the storm, and soon the water was completely calm. Then he asked the disciples why they were afraid and lacked faith.

Janet shared this story with our leadership team, and a sense of peace came over us as a ministry. Whenever somebody gave us more bad news or another team called to cancel, Janet would remind us all, "Jesus is in our boat. We're not going down."

May has always been our busiest month, but it was no surprise that in May 2009 we were flooded with cancellations. One of the only groups that didn't cancel was a company called Defenders. Based in Indiana, Defenders is an authorized premier provider for ADT Home Security Systems. Dave Lindsey and his wife, Jessica, had launched Defenders in 1998 out of their two-bedroom apartment, selling their Ford Explorer to help provide the startup capital. As the business grew larger, Dave and Jessica joined YPO and were eventually introduced to Homes of Hope in December 2007. Their family enjoyed the experience so much that the next year the Lindseys brought their management team through the Homes of Hope program. I flew to Indianapolis in 2008 to discuss with Dave and Jessica if Homes of Hope would potentially be a good fit for all their employees.

During dinner Dave and Jessica began to discuss a potential partnership with Defenders. Dave said to me, "The Homes of Hope experience was the mission trip I had always wanted to find for our family. Sean, tell me honestly, is there anything else out there that is better than Homes of Hope?" His question caught me a bit off guard. I paused for a moment to consider how to best respond.

"To be honest, I don't know of anything," I said with a big smile. "I mean, you spend a few days with your family building a home for another family living in poverty, knowing you're changing their lives. If there is something better than Homes of Hope out there that families can participate in, I haven't heard about it yet."

Dave took a few moments to soak in my comments. Then he sat back in his chair and declared, "Okay, I am in! We are going to start bringing our employees and their families through Homes of Hope. Jessica and I have learned that the things that impact us need to be shared with those we care about. I call it 'ever-expanding influence.' It's one of the core passions for our company."

As a result of our new partnership, Defenders had booked several trips, including one scheduled for May 2009, right in the midst of our "perfect storm." Defenders decided to hold steady and not cancel. By the time they arrived, the swine flu concerns had ended, and we had agreed to take the Defenders group to Ensenada, because it had no prior incidents of drug violence. On the way down to Ensenada, the Defenders group stopped by our new San Antonio del Mar property for a bathroom break and a quick tour of our new campus as it was being constructed. We had most of the infrastructure installed and four of thirty-six buildings completed.

As Dave and I walked the property together, he turned to me and said, "It must be tough having all of the groups canceling. How can I help you?"

My first inclination was to ask him for a big financial donation. But I knew that was short-sighted. I had watched on the news as the US government had begun a bailout program for the struggling auto industry, giving cash and loans. That kind of action works in the short-term but isn't sustainable. The only way for the auto industry to thrive again was to get people to buy new cars so they could manufacture more. Their purpose is to make cars and sell them, not to take bailout money.

I turned to Dave and said, "I am sure you could write us a check and keep us afloat for a while, but that is not what we exist for. YWAM San Diego/Baja exists to serve the poor and to disciple the nations. The most important thing we need right now is for groups to show up and build. That activity will keep us alive economically and, most important, help us fulfill our mission and vision."

Inspired by our conversation, Dave gathered his senior management team, and they did the math to figure out what would be the most houses they could do between May and the end of the year. As a result, they pledged to build thirty homes for the poor with their Defenders teams. Since 2009 was almost half over, this was an impressive commitment! Defenders followed through on their promise to build thirty homes, and we ended the year having completed 150 homes. The thirty homes Defenders built were 20 percent of our total for the year, and the economic impact of all the extra activity helped keep our organization alive.

Other partners of ours also stepped up to lend their support during our perfect storm. In the fall of 2009, I received an unsolicited call from one of our donors who had recently made a $68,000 donation to our property project to let me know that if I needed to use their donation for other purposes, we could. I also got another unsolicited call from a supporting church, Westside Kings, in Calgary, that informed me they were sending a $10,000 gift to be used for whatever we needed to help get through the crisis.

We were also reevaluating all our operations and cutting our overhead costs in whatever ways possible. At one of our board meetings, Mike Kemper pulled me aside and said, "I'm going to tell you this once, but you're probably not going to do it. Cut way deeper than you think you can and faster than you could ever imagine, and you'll find yourself popping out the other side of this tough time in one piece."

On a management level, we tried to implement what Mike recommended by making cuts in our overhead, but we kept thinking everything would get better soon. Optimism is generally a good trait to possess as a leader, but in a crisis you have to be brutally honest about the situation you are in. In hindsight, we should have made much deeper cuts and made them faster.

Our ministry was built to host six thousand people and build three hundred houses a year, and we found ourselves hosting only three thousand people and building only 150 homes, a 50 percent reduction in activity. We eventually sold half of our vehicle fleet and got rid of a lot of equipment we could live without. Many of our staff had to move out of some of the rental housing we had and squeeze in together in order to reduce our overhead. As for our San Diego offices, we went to our landlords and asked if we could move into a smaller unit for a reduced price. They agreed to work with us, and we soon moved into an office a few doors down in the same complex that was a third the size of our prior unit. Although we saved money by moving, we soon found ourselves jammed into what now seemed like a tiny space with boxes and desks stacked on top of each other.

As painful as they were, our cuts in overhead and the positive effect of having no debt on our new San Antonio del Mar property enabled us to stabilize the finances of our ministry by the middle of 2010.

Crises can also turn a ministry in unexpected, yet positive, new directions. Once again, a question would help nudge Homes of Hope toward a new path of growth. I received a call from Eric Affeldt, who at the time was the chairperson of the YPO Christian Network. The Christian Network had built homes with us between Christmas and New Year's since 1997.

"I have been getting calls from some of our members about what is going on in Mexico," Eric said. "We don't want to have to cancel our trip altogether, so can you find another place for us to go build homes besides Mexico?"

The YPO Christian Network was one of our best partners, and I didn't want to lose our connection with them. As Eric and I talked on the phone about what to do next, various data points suddenly clicked in my mind and a connection formed between Eric's question and a conversation I had a few months earlier with Giacomo Coghi, a YWAM leader in Costa Rica. Giacomo mentioned that he and his staff were interested in starting Homes of Hope in Costa Rica. He said the country's population was around 4.5 million people, but a million of them were economic refugees from Nicaragua, one of the poorest countries in Central America. Most were in desperate need of housing.

"How would you feel about going to Costa Rica?" I asked Eric over the phone. He responded that he was open to the idea but needed more details before he could say yes. I asked Eric to give me a few days to pull some of the details together, and then I immediately called Giacomo. He was indeed open to helping me pull off a Homes of Hope build in Costa Rica after Christmas. Giacomo was a key leader in YWAM's community development movement and was working with several impoverished communities that needed Homes of Hope. I learned there was a nice hotel near the airport that had rooms available for the group. So I got back to Eric, and we agreed we would switch the event from Mexico to Costa Rica.

The turnout for the Costa Rica build was smaller than normal, but there were still enough volunteers to construct two homes for the poor. Those who participated loved working in Costa Rica, and to our surprise, they all wanted to come back again in 2011. Within a month after the 2010 event was over, the 2011 event was fully booked! It was clear, even with our crisis in Mexico, that God was not finished with Homes of Hope, and we were about to explode into new nations with our movement.

Terry Snow, the YWAM director in Haiti, had contacted me in 2009 about starting Homes of Hope in that country. Nothing came of that conversation until January 2010 when a massive earthquake hit Haiti, killing 300,000 people and leaving more than a million homeless. Haiti is the poorest country in all of the Americas, and the tragedy made a terrible situation in many areas even worse. In response, over the next few years Terry and his courageous team would build almost two hundred homes for the poor.

Defenders also became a key partner in our Homes of Hope global expansion. What started with the Lindsey family attending a home build in Ensenada in 2007 eventually led to their whole company's involvement. Dave had such passion for Homes of Hope that I invited him to join our board of directors. During one of our meetings, he stressed the importance of Homes of Hope expanding into other countries.

"Even if the violence stops tomorrow, it will take a few years for some groups to feel comfortable building again in Mexico," Dave said.

"We all know eventually everything will get back to normal, but we should use this crisis to clarify what we are all about and look for new growth opportunities."

There were plenty of nodding heads in the room, as what Dave was saying made sense to everyone on the board. "What do you think about the Dominican Republic?" Dave asked. "There are plenty of people in need of housing there. It's near the East Coast and easy for groups to travel there."

I was open to expanding into new areas, but we needed the right leader in the Dominican Republic (DR) to make it a reality. Little did I know that God was already putting together an amazing plan for us to plant a new work in the DR. One of our emerging leaders from the Ensenada campus, Malcolm Taylor, had done a prior outreach in the DR, and God had given him a heart for that nation. I was delighted to learn that Malcolm had already developed a strategic plan to engage the Dominican Republic. Malcolm and I did a site visit to the DR to process the idea of starting a new YWAM work with the existing leadership there. We asked plenty of questions and ultimately identified the city of San Pedro as the right place to start a new YWAM/Homes of Hope ministry location.

During our perfect storm, in addition to Costa Rica, Haiti, and the DR, we were able to see Homes of Hope start in Jamaica, Panama, Chile, Brazil, and Cambodia. When groups contacted us with concerns about Mexico, we offered one of our other new locations as an alternative. Crisis does clarify, and it was clear that God wanted Homes of Hope to be a global movement impacting the poor.

Another kind of expansion came through the visionary leadership of Sam Kolias, a highly successful Canadian businessman who had done several Homes of Hope builds with his family. On one of Sam's family trips to work with us in Mexico, his daughter Isabella turned to him and said, "Dad, isn't Homes of Hope great? Don't you think everyone at Boardwalk would want to build a house?" Isabella's question inspired Sam to consider how he could engage his twelve hundred employees at Boardwalk in service to the poor. Sam wasted no time in contacting me.

"You know what, Sean?" Sam declared. "We don't just need Youth With A Mission; we also need *Companies* With A Mission." Sam's energy and enthusiasm were contagious.

I loved the idea of Companies With A Mission (CWAM) because it captured God's heart for the poor and also because I believe the real purpose of all business is to create work and wealth for all humanity. God does not just care about the poor; he cares about what happens in the sphere of the economy as well. Sam was so inspired by the CWAM concept that he flew to Kona, Hawaii, to share the idea with YWAM founder Loren Cunningham. I also conveyed the idea of CWAM to Dave Lindsey, since it seemed to fit what God was doing with his company.

Dave loved the name and wanted to know if he could use the CWAM name in his efforts to inspire other companies beyond his own to be engaged in Homes of Hope and other acts of service. Sam was delighted to share the CWAM name with any business leader who wanted to use it to inspire their companies to engage in serving others more. Just like my daughter Andrea's question about building a home for the bus people in 1990, Isabella's question to her dad, Sam, helped spark a new movement to mobilize businesses to engage in greater acts of service.

By 2012 the CWAM movement was starting to grow. That year the Super Bowl happened to be in Indianapolis, Indiana, Dave Lindsey's hometown. Dave invited me to attend the Athletes in Action Super Bowl breakfast that was held each year before the big game. At the event, Bart Starr, the Hall of Fame quarterback for the Green Bay Packers, would present the Man of the Year Award to a deserving NFL player. As the breakfast drew closer, Dave decided to have CWAM serve as the lead sponsor of the event. CWAM would have five minutes in front of everyone at the breakfast to share its overall vision and about Homes of Hope. As a bonus, my friend Mike Regan from Chicago was gracious enough to get me two tickets to the Super Bowl game, so I invited my dad to join me for the big weekend.

When the breakfast started, two thousand people were in attendance, including business leaders and NFL players past and present. On every table around the room there sat a CWAM invitation to join a future Homes of Hope build. Shortly after the breakfast started, a five-minute Homes of Hope video played, inviting everyone to join in a home build. I kept wondering how I had wound up in such a special moment. I had dropped out of college, worked with youth, and built homes for the poor. And now I was sitting in a room filled with business leaders and pro athletes at the Super Bowl breakfast, with my dad sitting next to me, watching a Homes of Hope video! (And by the way, going to the game with my dad the next day was pretty awesome too.)

The CWAM movement was helping Homes of Hope grow. Dave realized that not everyone in his company could go on a home build trip, so he wanted to expand the impact by getting people to serve locally as well as internationally. Defenders had for years done many local service days, typically centered on a project chosen by someone on the executive team. Everyone in the company would be told where and when to show up for a day of local service.

The Defenders leadership decided to flip the service concept from a top-down model to a bottom-up model. Employees would be free to choose where and when to serve and be given several paid days per year to do so. Defenders even created a contest in which the employees were encouraged to grab two or three other coworkers to serve a charity they were inspired by and then report on what they did via a short presentation or video. The winning presentations would receive an extra donation from Defenders for the charity they served.

As Dave attended the very first service awards luncheon, he was deeply touched by the presentations that were made. One employee, because of an economic hardship, had lived at a homeless shelter for a short period of time until he landed a job at Defenders. The employee had gone back to serve at the same homeless shelter that had served him in his time of need.

The Defenders service challenge had worked so well inside his company that Dave decided to create a Super Service Challenge that would inspire other companies to create a culture of serving. Dave and Jessica put up a million dollars in prize money and engaged the business community in New Orleans to get out and do acts of service. Drew Brees, quarterback for the New Orleans Saints, agreed to be a spokesman for the Super Service Challenge held just before the Super Bowl in New Orleans in 2013. The Lindseys had decided to give their million-dollar gift through the Drew Brees Foundation. Dave and Jessica stood off to the side while Drew presented the winners of the Super Service Challenge with a donation to their charity. They intuitively knew that if Drew gave out the money in New Orleans, it would have a greater influence than if they did it. I have several pictures on my iPhone of Dave and Jessica smiling from ear to ear as someone else gave away their money. While standing there, it hit me—God must feel the same delight when he gives us good gifts and resources and then watches as we give them away and share them with others.

Dave likes to say, "Profits in business are like blood in your body. You need them to stay alive, but they don't tell you who you are." Companies should not exist simply to make profits any more than our bodies exist just to make blood. Every company and individual needs to discover their true purpose beyond just making a profit.

In 2014 Defenders celebrated their two hundredth build with Homes of Hope. Since the first build in 2007, the company had engaged over five thousand employees, spouses, and children in serving the poor. Dave told me, "Homes of Hope has helped change Defenders from a company that gives, to a company of givers." It was easy to see how Homes of Hope was changing the lives of the poor, but I'd never realized how big the lasting impact of Homes of Hope would be in the sphere of business.[1]

---

1. To find out more about the CWAM movement in Canada and the United States, go to www.cwam.com. To find out more about the Super Service Challenge, go to https://superservice challenge.com/.

Sean at refugee camp in Thailand, January 1980

Puppet show at refugee camp

Sean and Janet's wedding

Sean at old bus that inspired the second Home of Hope, 1990

Before picture, Rosarito, Mexico

Before picture, Tijuana, Mexico

Meeting the family on the first day

Building the walls of a new Home of Hope

Lifting the walls of a new home

Teamwork lifting a wall

Completing the roof on a Home of Hope

Opening the door to a new home

Tears of joy at a home dedication

2000th Home of Hope team photo

Lambert family home build, December 2007

First building in Playas de Tijuana, Mexico, December 1989

San Antonio del Mar campus, 2002

San Antonio del Mar campus, 2009

YWAM Ensenada campus, 1998

YWAM Ensenada campus, 2005

Homes of Hope 25th anniversary celebration, May 2015

Sean and Janet with family at the 25th anniversary celebration

Sergio Gomez at the 25th anniversary celebration

Lambert family build, May 2015

Costa Rica Home of Hope, 2013

San Pedro, Dominican Republic

Home of Hope in Haiti

Home of Hope in Uganda

Home of Hope in Panama

SIXTEEN

God's Generosity

"I always knew there was a God. I just didn't know that he cared about me."

Josefina Guzman-Ochoa

A S Homes of Hope began to engage the large community of Antorcha, located just a few miles from our San Antonio del Mar campus in Tijuana, we noticed many of the children didn't attend primary school. This was mainly because many were new to Antorcha, and having moved into the area during the school year, they had missed the enrollment cut-off date. With the drop in Homes of Hope build projects in 2009, many of our staff had more time to focus on community-outreach initiatives. In Antorcha we began to run an afterschool program called the Walking Circle. The program helped fill the education gap in the community. For those who were already in school, extra tutoring helped them to become better students.

Our staff tutored the children in subjects such as math, reading, and geography while instilling in them three core principles: to love themselves, to love others, and to love God. As YWAM staff taught the children, they also noticed a number of the mothers who were standing close by the learning circle and listening in on the lessons being taught. YWAM staff soon realized that many of the mothers also had difficulty reading and writing, not to mention little or no concept of basic math. Once our staff recognized this need, they started classes for the parents. One of the most wonderful early results was that, for the first time, some of the mothers could write their own names! They were excited, because from then on they would be able to sign their children's school papers and other important documents.

Soon we were engaging more than one hundred primary-school-aged children on a weekly basis. The head principal of the nearby primary school marveled at the students' improved test scores and asked one of our staff what we were doing with the youth to make them such great learners. Another initiative was a mobile library bus that visited communities throughout the week and allowed the children or their parents to sign out books to read. In the end, what makes the Walking Circle and the library bus work are the relationships they create between our staff and the communities we serve. As I have learned, the best answers in life are always rooted in relationships. The library bus, math worksheets, paper, and pencils are important, but the most important thing is that someone has a relationship with the children and the parents and is encouraging them to learn and grow.

Our staff also host several family events each year. In October we organize a celebration called Operation Light, which conveys the idea of bringing the light of God into the community. In December we invite all the families of the Walking Circle to our campus for a Christmas dinner and a special program. In the summer, we arrange for families to take a day trip to the beach. Many of our staff were shocked to learn that the majority of these families we were serving had never been to the ocean, even though they lived just a few miles away from it.

One of the life-changing relationships at the Walking Circle happened through our daughter Andrea, who volunteers there. In September 2012 she was approached in class by a woman named Josefina Guzman-Ochoa. The woman said she urgently needed to talk. So Andrea found a coworker to take over her class and stepped to the side to talk. Josefina told Andrea her family was in a place of desperation. She said they lived in a shack about a mile from Antorcha. Because of the unhealthy living conditions, her husband, Eric Sr., had gotten sick and lost his job.

"There is no food left in our house to feed our two children, and I spent our last few pesos to buy candy I hoped to sell today in front of the school."

Andrea stepped forward and looked into the bucket Josefina was holding, still filled with simple candies.

"Nobody has bought a single piece of candy today, and I don't know what to do. Can you help me?"

The Guzman-Ochoa family had owned a successful small electronics business in Tijuana until someone broke into their store and stole everything they had. After the theft, rather than keep paying rent on the business and their apartment in the city, they decided to make a down payment on a piece of land that they could own. Eric Sr. found work as a security guard, and their intention was to build a nice home to live in when they got more money. When they moved onto the land, they had nothing and had to build their small shack out of scavenged building materials. A neighbor gave them a stove and some old dishes, and they found an old mattress at the dump to use for a bed.

It turned out that Josefina and her family had been on the waiting list to receive a Home of Hope, but when our perfect storm hit and teams started canceling, the list got longer and longer. They first heard about our organization after visiting neighbors who had received a new home. The home was beautiful in their eyes, freshly painted with a solid concrete floor, three windows, a door that locked, drywall, and electrical wiring with plugs and light switches. They were hopeful they could have a house like that, but month after month went by with no news of when it would be their turn.

Andrea took down Josefina's information and tried to lift her spirit by praying with her and her six-year-old son, Eric Jr. Andrea typically did not bring money with her to the Walking Circle as many people there asked her for money. Since she didn't want to lie, it was easier to tell those who asked for help that she did not have any money with her. That day as she was climbing into the van to go to the Walking Circle, the thought popped into her mind: "Take five dollars with you." At the time, Andrea wasn't sure why she needed the five dollars, but everything was now coming into focus as she stood listening to Josefina's heart-breaking story. Andrea pulled the five-dollar bill out of her pocket and gave it to Josefina.

"This is all I have right now, but we're going to help you," Andrea assured her. "Together we are going to figure this out."

A look of relief appeared on Josefina's face as tears welled up in her eyes. Eric looked up to his mother and said, "Now we will be able to have tortillas for dinner!"

Andrea was often approached by the poor in Mexico looking for help, but what resonated with her in this instance was Josefina's deep sincerity. She and her family had reached a place of utter desperation. Josefina did not present herself as if anyone owed her anything; she lacked hope and couldn't go on the way things were. Earlier that day her son Eric had been prodding his mom to go to the Walking Circle. "Mom, we have to find the Americans. I know they come to Antorcha every Tuesday, and they're going to help us." He bugged her all the way to school and then on the way home. Josefina didn't want to go to the Walking Circle. She was ashamed of her poverty. But because little Eric was so persistent, she ended up talking to Andrea.

Andrea left their meeting with a heavy heart. It is one thing to read about poverty but another to experience it relationally and up close from the perspective of a despairing mother.

The day Andrea met Josefina happened to fall on what our family calls Taco Tuesday. Each week we meet for dinner together at El Torritos restaurant. We were enjoying our chips and salsa and carne asada tacos when Andrea arrived, deeply moved by her encounter with Josefina. Over dinner she explained the situation. What touched me about Josefina's story is that she tried to sell candy and make the best of her situation. How many times do we think of the poor as being lazy and unmotivated, just waiting for the next handout? Josefina definitely wasn't lacking ambition or diligence. She cared about her kids and her husband. She had invested all the money she had to buy candies to sell so her family could eat.

Even before we finished dinner, Janet, Rachel, and Andrea decided to go to Walmart and load up on food for the Guzman-Ochoa family. There was no way they could sit in a nice restaurant enjoying dinner, knowing Josefina's family had no food to eat. While checking out at Walmart, Rachel and Andrea refused to let Janet pay for all the food. They wanted to be a part of giving to the Guzman-Ochoa family.

The next day, Janet, Andrea, and Rachel, along with some of our other staff, set out to deliver the food they had purchased. None of the people in the car had been to Josefina's house, so they had to follow a less-than-precise list of directions scrawled on a piece of notebook paper provided by Alfonso, one of our builders. After a few wrong turns and help from some neighbors, they motored up a steep, rain-soaked hill in a four-wheel-drive vehicle and found the place.

As they pulled up in front of Josefina's ramshackle, dirt-floored home, she ran toward the car with tears streaming down her cheeks. She had no idea why they had come, nor did she know they had brought food and supplies for her and her family. She was simply happy to see Andrea's smiling face again. As she hugged Andrea, Josefina told her, "I always knew there was a God, but until now I never knew he cared about me."

When they brought the food inside, they could see for the first time the desperate living conditions of the Guzman-Ochoa family. As they visited with Josefina, she mentioned another dream beyond having a home. She had been struggling to send Eric Jr. to a private school. The cost was the equivalent of only ten US dollars a month, and the school sometimes allowed her to clean the classrooms to help cover the tuition. The school was about an hour-long bus ride from their home. To save money after dropping off her son at school, she would often wait all day near the property and then pick him up when school ended to take the bus home again.

"If I never eat yogurt again or have a new dress in my life, that's okay as long as my children get a good education," Josefina told them.

It took a few months, but the Guzman-Ochoa family finally got a new Home of Hope, built by a group of students from the Schulich School of Engineering at the University of Calgary. Sam Kolias, a UC graduate, had made the build possible long before he knew about the Guzman-Ochoa family. Sam partnered with Lynne Cowe Falls, a Schulich faculty member, to encourage UC engineering students to participate in a Homes of Hope trip. Sam told Lynne, "If you round up twenty students who are willing to pay one hundred dollars, I will cover all of the other expenses for them to go to Mexico and build a Home of Hope for the poor." Lynne put out the word about Sam's offer, announcing that the first twenty students to show up at her office at eight o'clock in the morning with their passports and $100 would get to go on the trip. To Lynne's surprise, she found *fifty* eager students lined up in front of her office, some having spent all night waiting in line for the opportunity to serve the poor in Mexico. When Sam heard the news, he agreed, along with Trico Homes out of Calgary, to fund *two* houses instead of one so that every student who wanted to participate in Homes of Hope could do so.

As the vans of volunteers rolled up to the Guzman-Ochoas' property at the start of the first day of building, Josefina, surrounded by her family, stood in front of everyone and spoke to the group.

"I pray that God would always bless you in every moment. We are never going to forget this day. We will always have it in our minds. And to each one of you, we are going to have you in our hearts. Thank you."

As the students and our YWAM builders began construction on the home, Josefina found Andrea and told her, "I don't want this day to end, because it is so exciting to see this happening. We have been living on dirt with just a few shaky walls around us, and now we are going to have a beautiful house."

As the construction on the Guzman-Ochoas' home came to a close on the second day of the build, the students from the University of Calgary surprised Josefina and her children by taking them to the store to buy groceries and other supplies. Although it was a joyous occasion, the intensity of the moment soon overcame Josefina. As she walked down the rows of oatmeal, cereal, and other breakfast items, she began sobbing. Eric Sr. approached and gently wrapped his arms around her. When the group asked Josefina what was wrong, she could barely speak.

Through the interpreter, she told them that every morning she always tried to make sure there was something for her husband and children to eat before they went to work and school. "When we were out of food, sometimes I would go to the outdoor food markets to pick up discarded vegetables and fruit. It was always such a struggle."

What Josefina didn't say was that she had not eaten breakfast in as long as she could remember. Now she was standing in front of an overflowing shopping cart. The sight of her cart full of food had brought back some of the painful memories of her family's daily fight to survive. Her tears were both tears of remembrance and tears of joy. God was now answering her prayers and answering them in abundance.

By the time the Guzman-Ochoa family returned to the build site, the construction had been completed and it was time for Josefina and Eric Sr. to take the keys and unlock the door to their family's new home. After opening the door, Josefina paused for a moment. Her husband put an arm around her shoulder, and, together with their two children, they stepped into their new house.

Their young daughter found her way back into the bedroom and pointed at the new bunk bed covered with blankets, clothing, and a few children's toys. "Look, Mommy! Look!" she yelled.

"Did you see your new bed?" Eric Sr. asked his son. "And you have clothes and a stuffed animal and a table. Did you see?"

Young Eric answered back with a huge smile as tears of happiness streamed down Josefina's face. After so many years of living in a moldy shack, their family finally had a real home.

When Andrea returned the next day, Josefina took her by the hand and explained that she wanted to do something for the other women with whom she had scavenged for food at the outdoor markets. Together with Andrea, Josefina put together seventeen bags of food out of what she had just received from the Schulich team the previous day. Josefina appreciated what she was given, but she was living with the painful memory of her friends having to scavenge for food that other people throw away. Josefina wanted her friends to feel the same joy and blessing that she was feeling. For her, it was exciting to give to others in need even if it meant she had less for herself.

The Guzman-Ochoas immediately started making improvements on the house, such as setting a perimeter of rocks to edge and outline their front yard. They even built a small room off the front of their house where Josefina could have a hair salon, as she had been trained in cutting hair and doing nails. They also constructed a room for an expanded kitchen. They used similar building materials to those used by the Homes of Hope team and even found paint that matched their existing house! They also built a little granny flat in the back for Josefina's mom to sleep in when she came to visit for several months at a time. It seemed that every time Andrea returned to the Guzman-Ochoa household, there was something new that they had been working on.

Andrea stayed in contact with the family and took the kids shopping for school supplies. By the next school year, they had saved enough money to buy their own supplies and no longer needed Andrea's help. It was easy to see that something had been sparked in their spirits, and they were no longer living in crisis mode.

Josefina had decided to attend one of our community discipleship programs called Envia, the Spanish word for "send," which was held at our San Antonio del Mar campus. Envia is a ten-week discipleship course that meets three times per week. The course helps students to know God more and teaches them how to apply their faith on a daily basis.

After Josefina attended the course, she was excited by how much she had grown spiritually and wanted Eric Sr. to have the same opportunity. She was hungry to learn more about God and how she could serve him with all her heart. Eric Sr. joined in the next Envia. They soon began considering joining one of our upcoming Discipleship Training Schools (DTS). This would be a big leap for them because the DTS was an intensive five-month school that required them to quit their jobs to be full-time students.

Eric and Josefina asked the pastors of their church to pray with them about attending the DTS, and during the prayer time, God spoke to Josefina and gave her the reassurance she was looking for. "All that you have is a gift. Trust me with all these things I have given you," he said.

It was a big step of obedience, but everything began falling into place for them to attend the school. To pay for the school, they sold some of their personal items and found a renter to live in their house while they were gone. YWAM was also able to provide some financial help through a student scholarship fund.

Eric and Josefina completed their DTS, graduating in August 2014, and decided to join YWAM full-time as official staff members of

YWAM San Diego/Baja! Just a few years ago they were destitute, and now they are full-time missionaries working in our Homes of Hope family selection department. The pain of their prior life is for them a point of compassion, understanding, and insight as they interview new families applying for a home of their own. Josefina also works with the Walking Circle, where she first met Andrea.

The Guzman-Ochoas are committed to continuing to grow in the Lord and to helping other families in need. They are living proof that God can change families. If God can change a family, then there is hope that we can see a community transformed. And if there is hope for a community, then we can have hope for the transformation of whole nations.[1]

1. To see a video about the Guzman-Ochoa family story, go to www.ywamhomesofhope .org/ochoa.

SEVENTEEN

Communities of Hope

"God's mercy and grace give me hope—for myself, and for our world."
Billy Graham

MAY 2015 marked the twenty-fifth anniversary of Homes of Hope, and months before the event our leadership began to discuss how we could celebrate it. Mike Lantz, one of our board members, suggested we build twenty-five homes for the poor in one weekend—one new home to symbolize each year of Homes of Hope. I loved the idea, but Janet and a few other staff members thought it was a bit crazy to think we could build that many homes over a single weekend. At that point, the most homes we had ever built in one weekend was thirteen. The more I thought about building twenty-five homes, the more God's grace came upon me to go for it.

I rallied our staff, and we started working on all the details, including mobilizing the five hundred volunteers it would take to construct that many houses. We also made a strategic decision that several of the houses would be built by Mexicans, many of whom were prior Homes of Hope recipients. We wanted to bring everything full circle by giving them an opportunity to serve another family in need. I was also happy that one of the homes was going to be built by my family. My mom and dad agreed to come, along with my brother, my six sisters, and most of their spouses and children. The plan was to build fifteen homes for families in Tijuana and ten in Ensenada with the weekend culminating in a grand celebration on our sports field at the San Antonio del Mar campus.

During the anniversary weekend, both at our Ensenada campus and at our San Antonio del Mar campus, we set aside time in the mornings and evenings to gather together to remember our favorite Homes of Hope stories. One of the people I asked to share remembrances was Dave Stone, who, along his wife, Trina, had participated in fifty-three home builds since 1997.

Dave told of a Homes of Hope trip his company had done with their sales and marketing team. "When we arrived at the build site, it had been raining for days. Our team sat in the vans staring out at the sheets of rain hammering the already flooded patch of land. We didn't think there was any way we would be able to start working, but we patiently waited in the vans hoping the rain would stop soon. But it didn't. We figured it would be best to return to the YWAM campus and wait to see if the weather conditions improved the next day."

Our assembled group of three hundred staff and volunteers were quickly drawn in by Dave's story.

"As we were getting ready to leave, I noticed our YWAM host standing out in the rain consoling a young woman with her two children. I couldn't help but notice how upset she was when she was told our group was preparing to leave. I got out of the van, and our host explained to me that the woman's father had said she was crazy to believe someone was going to give her a new house. In fact, he thought she was so crazy that he had already taken one of her children from her and was threatening to come take the other two kids away as well. Our host told me, 'If this Home of Hope isn't built, her family is going to be ripped apart.'"

Dave's voice choked with emotion as he recalled walking back to the vans with a renewed perspective and determination. "I told our team, 'We are getting out of these vans, and we are going to build this family a house!'"

Despite the difficult conditions, his team set to work. At the end of the second day, they completed the build, and the woman's family was welcomed into their new home. Dave said, "I was able to reconnect with her a few months later at the San Antonio del Mar campus and was thankful to find her accompanied by another family member, her father. After he had seen firsthand what Homes of Hope had done for his daughter and his grandkids, he was deeply touched. She soon led him to the Lord. I know that each volunteer's presence at a build site is an answer to someone's prayer and a visible extension of God's grace and love to them."

Drew Smith, a former board member who had participated in thirty-one builds, also shared about a favorite memory of Homes of Hope. He recalled the last words of the Old Testament in Malachi 4: "He will turn the hearts of the parents to their children, and the hearts of the children to their parents." Drew noted that these words were repeated in the book of Luke to emphasize the work that God does in our lives in the area of family. "I am thankful for all the hearts of children that have been turned back to their parents through the Homes of Hope program. I will never forget when we handed the keys over to the mother of a receiving family. She said, 'Now my children will never have to sleep outside again.'"

Drew told another story of a time when his team traveled to a desolate area of Tijuana where they found a few rusted-out cars but saw no signs of a shelter or dwelling: "As I wondered where the family was living, a car door swung open. A moment later, a young mother named Maria stepped out of the car holding her newborn infant. She had been living in the back of an old station wagon and had given birth in that same vehicle only two weeks before our build team arrived. On the back of the station wagon, she had hung a sheet with the words written in Spanish, 'Thank you, God, for bringing these special people to us.'"

Drew said he also often thought about the number of current YWAM staff members who had received a Home of Hope as children and were now helping other families get a home. "I appreciate the impact Homes of Hope had on my children and the children of many other volunteers who witnessed faith in action through their parents. Faith is based not only on what one says or believes but on *what one does*. Homes of Hope is a great conduit to allow us to demonstrate our faith."

Drew's point about the value of family resonated with me. Each year, thousands of Mexican men and women illegally cross the border to seek work in the United States. We don't often think about the heavy price these families pay to send their husbands or wives off in search of jobs in the United States. They face many dangers on the journey north. Once they do find work, they send money home, but what is the relational cost to the spouses, to the sons and daughters who need a father or mother in their lives as they grow up? The price paid by everyone crossing the border illegally is way higher than we often think. My good friend Stan Marek once said to me, "Every time I build a Home of Hope, it's one less Mexican man or woman who will have to leave their family and make the perilous journey to the United States to find work."

The house building aspect of the twenty-fifth anniversary weekend went off without a hitch; our staff did an amazing job organizing everything. YWAM founders Loren and Darlene Cunningham were able to join us, and when Sunday afternoon rolled around, we were all ready to celebrate. To kick off the event, we honored the nation of Mexico with a special flag ceremony, and then Pastor Carlos Perea from Playas de Tijuana, a good friend of our ministry for many years, opened our celebration in prayer.

Pastor Carlos prayed, "Heavenly Father, we give you glory and honor, and we thank you for these more than five thousand homes that have been built. Thank you for the more than 100,000 volunteers that have given their time and talents to Homes of Hope over the years. Many years ago, Lord, we prayed that people would come from the east, west, north, and south to join us. We declared not only that this location would be a missionary base but that it would be a fountain of blessings where springs of living water would come out and bless the people of Mexico and the nations. We are very grateful for what you have done, and we want to join together in celebration because you have always been there for us. As one body, Youth With A Mission, Homes of Hope, and every single volunteer here today, we give you all of the glory, all of the praise. Thank you, Lord Jesus. Thank you for using us. Amen."

The afternoon celebration served as an ideal opportunity to invite many of the individuals who shaped Homes of Hope to share a few words. As part of the main celebration event, I asked Dave Gustaveson to share about the first offering to Jesus taken back in January 1990 that had led to the building of the first house. Robert and Jill Kulhawy shared their part in helping us engage with business leaders and their families.

Sergio Gomez, the man who influenced me to build my first home for the poor, also made an appearance. Without Sergio there would be no Homes of Hope story to tell, and I was honored to be able to recognize his role that day in front of the celebration crowd. The money to build the first home back in 1990 may have come from our offering to Jesus, but the heart and passion for building for the poor came from Sergio. God had put it on my heart to give Sergio a love offering of one dollar for every Home of Hope he had inspired us to build. I was smiling from ear to ear as I handed him a big envelope filled with $5,000 in cash. Sergio was gracious in accepting our ministry's love gift, and he grinned as I handed him the microphone.

"You know, I haven't seen Sean in many years," Sergio said, "but I have a picture on my desk of the two of us standing together that I look at often. I have seen firsthand what YWAM has been able to accomplish for this city. YWAM came to this region at the right time with the right people and has been the face of Jesus to the people here in Baja. I could preach you a sermon today because I am a pastor, but the sermon that I know that speaks the longest is when I build a home and give the keys to a family in need."

My favorite moment of the celebration was standing on the stage with my family. My daughter Andrea and I shared a special moment as she told her part in the story of inspiring me to build the second house. Our oldest daughter, Rachel, and her husband, John, joined us with their three children, Parker, Aviana, and Paxton. Rachel and John serve full-time with us at YWAM San Diego/Baja and oversee all our training programs. They are actively preparing the next generation of Homes of Hope workers.

Andrea was joined by her husband, Guy, and daughter, Alexa. Andrea provides leadership in many areas of our ministry. Guy, a professional cyclist, started a nonprofit organization called Hope Sports, with a motto of "Engaging athletes to bring hope to the world." Through Hope Sports, Guy has mobilized hundreds of professional and Olympic athletes to participate in Homes of Hope builds. Tiffany, our youngest daughter, is passionate about communications and photography. She loves to amplify the voice of the poor and to show and tell the story of God at work around the world.

Our twenty-fifth anniversary celebration wouldn't have been complete without hearing from our founders, Loren and Darlene. Their visionary leadership and encouragement have made room for millions of young people all around the world to be a part of YWAM's missions movement. Janet and I are so thankful they made room for us. We are privileged to multiply the vision of waves of young people here in Mexico.

Near the end of the celebration I shared my thoughts about our next twenty-five years and a new Communities of Hope vision. In prior Homes of Hope leaders' meetings, God had shown us that Homes of Hope was our gateway into the communities we serve, but now we were to expand our vision to engage communities on many other levels and areas of need. The primary template for the Communities of Hope vision comes from a document Loren Cunningham created in 1981, titled "The Christian Magna Carta" (available in the back of this book). Communities of Hope is also influenced by Loren's vision to impact what we in YWAM call the "seven spheres of society"—family, religion, government, economy, education, communications, and arts and sports. Through the Communities of Hope vision, we would engage impoverished communities around the world on many levels in order to see real transformational change take place.

In 1990 Homes of Hope was our only program. It's where we started and how we entered into communities and built trust. I believe our next twenty-five years will involve a much bigger picture of how we can impact whole communities on multiple levels. In each community we serve, we will first do a baseline assessment of their present resources, both strengths and weaknesses. We will then develop a customized strategy to serve their real needs and see transformation take place in that community.

Through Communities of Hope, we will address both the spiritual and practical needs of impoverished communities around the world in an integrated way. I believe God wants us to keep building homes, but he's also leading us to be comprehensive and well-rounded in the way we serve families and communities.

The Communities of Hope vision is also being strengthened through innovations and new technologies. In many developing nations, deforestation is a huge problem, so we look for alternatives to wood in building homes for the poor. Concrete blocks are not the best choice, because they are often poorly manufactured in the developing world, and it takes a long time to build a house with them. In southern Mexico we use metal studs, and in other parts of the world we use a technology called Insulated Core Foam (ICF) blocks, which look like giant Legos and can be put together easily by volunteer teams to build an amazing home. Along with the ICF blocks, builders only need concrete, mortar, and rebar, which are available in almost every developing nation. The insulation rating on the ICF blocks for both heat and cold is outstanding—far better than concrete. We are embracing other innovative technologies in the areas of sanitation, clean water, solar energy, and food security.

As we closed our twenty-fifth anniversary celebration time, we took an offering. The money raised would be used to build more homes for the poor around the world. God had blessed the first offering back in 1990 in a remarkable way, and I was full of faith to see what God would do with this offering over the next twenty-five years. One of our staff had brought orange Home Depot buckets with the words "Let's do this" printed on the side. We used those buckets to collect the offering. When all of the donations and pledges were counted, $75,000 was raised for the poor!

Looking back at our twenty-fifth celebration, it was a big blur of activity and people. I wish I could have been two people on that day: one person who was making it special for everyone who attended and another person who could just sit back, reflect, and take it all in. Building twenty-five homes for the poor in one weekend had a tremendous positive impact on our staff, and we gained confidence that God could do more through us than we could ever envision for ourselves.[1]

Our future as a ministry is bright, but we can expect that other storms and growth challenges will hit us from time to time. We must

1. To see a short video on the twenty-fifth anniversary Homes of Hope celebration, go to www.ywamhomesofhope.org/25th.

always remember that Jesus is in our boat, and he is with us during every storm and every growth challenge. To continue to grow our ministry, I have also recognized the need to keep growing myself as a leader.

At one of our Homes of Hope events, I had an opportunity to talk with Dave Browne, the former CEO of LensCrafters, about organizational growth and leadership.

"Dave, how did you do it? How did you grow LensCrafters into a billion-dollar-a-year company?" I asked.

Dave responded, "I had to change my leadership style from 'do and tell' to 'coach and develop.'"

His words described my own leadership journey over twenty-five years. When I first started YWAM San Diego/Baja in 1991, I did everything. I answered the phone, booked new teams, made bank deposits—and since I was always in a hurry, I just told our staff what to do next. My entire leadership style was "do and tell." I was not coaching and developing our staff in those early years. Things changed at YWAM San Diego/Baja as I became intentional about coaching and developing our staff. I am so grateful for the new generation of leaders God is raising up for our ministry. I want to continue growing and coaching and developing others.

Janet and I give all glory and honor to God for his leadings, provision, and grace that have kept us going all these years. We also give thanks for all those who invested, sacrificed, and joined in the journey with us. We serve a God of hope, and hope is a powerful tool in transforming the lives of individuals, families, and communities.

"May the God of hope fill you with all joy and peace as you trust in him, so that you may overflow with hope by the power of the Holy Spirit" (Romans 15:13).

Go, Serve, Transform

HOMES of Hope is fast approaching six thousand homes built for the poor in twenty-three countries around the world. On average, one new Home of Hope is being built every day somewhere in the world. An estimated thirty thousand people have received shelter, and the total value given to the poor is over $55 million. I regularly get requests from our YWAM family around the world about helping to start a new Homes of Hope program in their city or nation.

Often I am brought to tears when I reflect back on my first home build in May 1990. I marvel at how God used an offering from a small group of unsalaried YWAM missionaries and an inspired question from a three-year-old girl to create this global housing movement. Because of our positive impact on the poor, we have been honored by the Mexican government and gained some amazing media and ministry recognition.

At its core, the Homes of Hope story is about the power of servant leadership. It's also about discovering God's leadings and then responding with faith and obedience. I believe it's important to acknowledge that processing and understanding God's leadings and guidance is a relational process and one that is also subjective. Just putting God's name on something does not make it his will. In my younger years I told a girl, "God wants us to date." Then three weeks later I told her, "God wants us to break up." I am pretty sure God had nothing to do with either of these "leadings," but I was spiritually immature and decided to slap God's name over what I wanted. It takes an honest and humble heart, a desire to be in close friendship with God, and faith to believe God can speak to you to truly hear his voice.

A few years ago we adopted a core slogan for YWAM San Diego/ Baja: "Go, Serve, Transform." *Go* is about movement and mobilization; it's about making room for others to be involved in serving the spiritually and physically needy of our world. *Serve* is what we do; we serve the poor, the lost, and the least of these. *Transform* is both our end goal and our commitment to the people we serve. Transformation is about discipleship, mentoring, coaching, and teaching others. We are called to *make* disciples, not find them.

I invite you to consider joining us in our long-term Communities of Hope vision. You could mobilize a group to build a home for a family in need. You could join us as a volunteer; we need cooks, landscapers, builders, translators, and maintenance people who are willing to work behind the scenes to support what we do. If you want to get really radical in following Jesus, consider attending one of our five-month Discipleship Training Schools and then joining us as a full-time staff member. Does God have a call on your life to engage a broken world?

Perhaps you could also consider sending in a donation to help support the Homes of Hope movement. We will put your resources to good use in our Communities of Hope vision. Your gift will help us to throw a few more love-your-neighbor parties around the world.

Acknowledgments

Thank you . . .

To my wife, Janet. Together we have discovered God's destiny and call for our lives, and together we will continue to walk out that calling. I love you.

To my three daughters, Rachel, Andrea, and Tiffany, who are embedded in the foundations of the Homes of Hope story. You are true partners with us in this vision.

To my parents, Jim and Nancy Lambert, who raised me to love God and love people.

To Loren and Darlene Cunningham for making room for Janet and me to be "youth with a mission."

To John Dawson for seeing what I could be and not what I was.

To Chris and Jane Crane for being the first to receive us when we moved to the San Diego/Baja area and for walking with us in close friendship and support through all these years.

To Dave and Jessica Lindsey for believing in the book project and helping to resource it in a significant way.

To Adam Mitchell, my writing partner in this project. Your professionalism, writing skills, and contribution in arranging the story line were vital to getting the book completed.

To Patrick Butler for your early interview work that helped pull the story out of Janet and me and others. To Janet Butler for taking time to pray over this project.

To Kim Majors for your help as a researcher in providing supporting content for the book.

To Scott Tompkins for your significant editorial work on the book.

To my sisters, Julia Frericks and Rosie Lambert, and my mother, Nancy Lambert, who all gave feedback and input on the book.

To Marcia Zimmermann for your editorial contributions to the book.

To the Carroll family, who were the first to give to the book project, and to Phil Carroll, who cheered me on in my journey of serving the poor like no one else I have ever met. Phil, I wish you were still here to see this book project come to pass, but I know you're watching from heaven.

To our YWAM family, all of the staff and volunteers, past and present, who have given themselves so freely to love God and serve the poor. This is your story too.

To all of those who have joined the Homes of Hope movement since 1990. There would be no Homes of Hope story without your contribution and generous sacrifice of time, talents, and resources. Thank you for showing up.

Most importantly, I thank God for the awesome privilege he gives each of us to know him and partner with him in the discovery of what it means to love our neighbor. He is the full explanation for my life and for the Homes of Hope movement.

The Christian Magna Carta

We affirm the Christian Magna Carta, which describes the following basic rights as implicit in the gospel. Everyone on earth has the right to:

- Hear and understand the gospel of Jesus Christ.
- Have a Bible available in his/her own language.
- Have a Christian fellowship available nearby, to be able to meet for fellowship regularly each week, and to have Biblical teaching and worship with others in the body of Christ.
- Have a Christian education available for their children.
- Have the basic necessities of life: food, water, clothing, shelter, and health care.
- Lead a productive life of fulfillment spiritually, mentally, socially, emotionally, and physically.
- We commit ourselves, by God's grace, to fulfill this covenant and to live for his glory.

Developed by Youth With A Mission's Global Leadership Team in 1981

Contact and Resources

For additional information about Homes of Hope around the world, visit our website at www.ywamhomesofhope.org.

For additional information about YWAM San Diego/Baja, our Mission Adventures program, or University of the Nations courses and seminars, visit the YWAM San Diego/Baja website at www.ywamsdb.org.

To send a gift to help a needy family receive a new home through Homes of Hope:

Online Credit Card Donations
Go to "Give" at www.ywamsdb.org.
In the note box, indicate your gift is for
"The Homes of Hope Scholarship Fund."

U.S. Check Donations
Make checks payable to *YWAM San Diego/Baja*
Mail to:
YWAM San Diego/Baja
P.O. Box 5417
Chula Vista, CA 91912 – USA

Canada Cheque Donations
Make cheques payable to *YWAM Society*
Mail to:
YWAM Society (Baja and Beyond)
P.O. Box # 1574
Cochrane, AB T4C1B5 – Canada
Make sure to include a note with your gift that your contribution is
for "The Homes of Hope Scholarship Fund."

Contact Information
info@ywamsdb.org
+1 619-420-1900

Buy a Book, Help Build a Home!

The Homes of Hope Story is an inspiring book that amplifies the voice of the poor, reveals servant-leadership principles, and invites the reader to join in and become part of the Homes of Hope movement. For every book purchased, a contribution will be made to the Homes of Hope scholarship fund, helping ensure another family in need gets a new home.

Is there a family member, friend, or coworker you want to share *The Homes of Hope Story* with?

Are you a group leader bringing a team to build with Homes of Hope? Get this book for each member of your team, or use it as a thank-you gift for those who support your endeavor.

To order additional copies of the book, go to
www.thehomesofhopestory.com

Inspire Your Group

To invite Sean Lambert, founder of Homes of Hope, to speak at your church or company event, email hohstory@gmail.com.